FLAT TOP RANCH
The Story of a Grassland Venture

FLAT TOP

THE STORY OF A

Edited by B. W. Allred and J. C. Dykes

RANCH

GRASSLAND VENTURE

By Louis Bromfield,
    C. C. Booth, B. W. Allred, Martine Emert,
    J. C. Dykes, G. O. Hedrick, W. B. Roberts,
    Charles Pettit, W. R. Van Dersal, and
    Frank Reeves

WILDSIDE PRESS

Library of Congress Catalog Card Number: 57-7332

PREFACE

THE IDEA of a book about my grassland venture, Flat Top Ranch, originated with Louis Bromfield. He offered to edit it and to contribute two chapters on the general purpose of the ranch and the progress that has been made on it. But as so often happens in human affairs, death intervened, and the book which Louis Bromfield had projected was brought to its final stages by J. C. Dykes and B. W. Allred, who had been enlisted to present certain technical phases for which they were admirably suited. They happily carried the original idea to fruition.

It was then suggested that I prepare a preface, but some of the comments in the book made this task hardly becoming of a modest man. I was, however, persuaded to attempt it, in the interest of presenting the Flat Top idea to the public. My reluctance remains, but here is my story.

I was lucky because I grew up on a ranch in the days before the big "plow-up" when most Texans ranched with plenty of grass on their spreads. I had seen literally a sea of grass in parts of Texas during my boyhood. From that time on I wanted a good ranch stocked with fine cattle, and in 1938 I felt I was able to buy and develop such a place, so I began to devote my time to buying and developing Flat Top Ranch.

Ranching can be an inspiring and time-consuming business if it's done right, and the study, planning, and management required can only be done by a man who lives on the ranch and devotes most of his attention to it.

Many who attain wealth seek the earthiness and freedom that they believe owning a ranch will give, but their ventures usually fail to give them the personal pleasure and financial rewards they want unless they live on the ranch and build for permanence. The hobby ranchers who want private fishing and hunting for entertainment or weekend lodges for family and friends seldom improve the basic ranching resources.

Too often they buy expensive ranches, then stock them and hire low-salaried foremen to run them. Usually, and particularly when there is a profit-sharing arrangement, the foreman overstocks the grass and does little to build up or maintain the soil, grass, water developments, fences, and buildings. These hobby ranchers usually are well-meaning men who merely lack the instincts and vision necessary to build for permanence and profit.

When I began looking for a ranch to buy in 1936, ranching was a lot different from what it had been when I formed my opinions about it as a boy in Archer County, Texas, where large operators ran their herds on unfenced grassy prairies. As land settlement progressed, many large ranches were halved, quartered, and re-subdivided, and much land was plowed and cropped.

The Texas land ownership pattern in 1938 wasn't much different from that of 1954, when there were 293,000 farms and ranches in Texas. Farm and ranch population was 1,-

141,000, meaning that there was an average of four people per farm and ranch. At present about thirteen out of one hundred Texans live on the land, and of these holdings there are 126,000 with fewer than one hundred acres, about 126,000 with one hundred to five hundred acres, and 41,000 with over five hundred acres.

Since there was never any federal homesteading in Texas, the ownership pattern was not always like this. But land-hungry people offered prices that the ranch and big-farm owners couldn't resist. So the big units were broken up and the division of land between two or more heirs on the death of an owner further reduced the size of the operating units.

This impractical pattern of ownership resulted in too many undersized, starvation farms and ranches, with consequent overplowing and overgrazing until the soil of the cropland became exhausted and eroded and the formerly excellent grassland deteriorated to poor condition. There was not enough cropland or grassland to provide the family with even a fair living, let alone enough to maintain pride and respectability. Hundreds of these units have been abandoned and many others are merely lived on by owners or tenants who earn their living elsewhere.

I decided to buy a number of these run-down and neglected farms plus the seven-thousand-acre Flat Top Ranch and develop this new holding into a productive cattle ranch. Thus I could have the ranch I had always wanted and at the same time help rebuild a worthwhile Texas resource. I have made considerable money from the natural resources of the Southwest. While thus engaged I have observed many others making much more money than I from oil, gas, and minerals. These resources that come from strata deeply bedded beneath the surface of the earth took millions of years to make and once exhausted cannot be renewed. I hope these men will come to believe as I do and will do something to replenish our renewable resources of soil, grass, and water in partial payment for the fortunes made while exhausting our sub-surface resources. They can do this by improving run-down land, planting forests, developing good pastures and ranges, improving natural homes for wildlife, and restoring watersheds. They can liquidate a debt to the country by rebuilding renewable resources, which itself rewards a man financially for his efforts. Furthermore, there is more personal satisfaction in accomplishing such ends than in trying to become a second Standard Oil Company.

A man with a large outside income can make many ranch improvements at little real cost to himself because the government allows a charge-off against income tax for ranch developments. The cost of stock tanks, brush control, and other developments, as well as depreciation against fences, buildings, and equipment are legitimate charge-offs against income tax.

I believe that in the Southwest grass is a more valuable resource than oil. We are exhausting the oil, but grass is perpetual when we treat it right. Unfortunately, grass has been thinned out or killed in some places by people who ran more hungry animals than they had grass for. Most of our ranges are in poor or fair condition when they should be kept in good and excellent condition.

These ranges can be restored, and this job of reclaiming

them is largely one of letting the native grasses come back naturally under resting or light grazing. The job is not so much one of getting two blades of grass to grow where one blade used to grow as it is of re-establishing one vigorously growing blade. My prescription is to have more grass than livestock, then both do their best. We have a lot of Johnsongrass fields where some of the cattle graze in summer while part of the native grasses rest in order to increase their root span and to develop seed.

There are ten million acres of Texas land in abandoned fields that produce little of value, and some grow worse from neglect each year. Water and wind erosion have removed part, and in places all, of the topsoil. These are critical silt source areas when it rains, and the wind blows the soil away when the weather is dry.

My ranch had several hundred acres of this kind of land which have been treated and seeded to grass to protect the soil and to provide grazing for my Herefords. A lot of this land was first seeded to legumes, which conditioned the soil for grass after a year or two. Native grass seed was then planted, and it took three to five years for the new stand to thicken and strengthen enough for safe grazing. It must be given time to take hold. Many good stands have been plowed up the first year after planting because the young grass looked scarce and puny.

Our native grasses—bluestems, Indiangrass, switchgrass, sideoats grama, and Texas wintergrass—are ideally suited to our conditions and the cattle like them and stay fat on them all year.

Several introduced grasses have been tried on the ranch,

but I like the natives best. When these outside grasses are used, they should be planted in fairly pure stands and fenced so they can be grazed by themselves. King Ranch (K.R.) bluestem is a popular introduction into Texas, and while it does well on the ranch, cattle prefer the natives, which finally crowd out the K. R. bluestem. Dallisgrass is another good one for lowlands and subirrigated areas. Cattle like it fine, but it is soon replaced as native grasses increase. Johnsongrass is an excellent cropland grass, but must be cultivated or it is replaced by natives. Bermudagrass is productive on deep soils and yields well in combination with the true clovers or button clover (a medic). It is considerably less palatable than our native grasses, which shade it out if they are not kept mowed or grazed out.

You will be surprised how responsive your soil will be to good treatment. Try a small experiment of your own and find out for yourself. It won't cost much to try and the result will be very rewarding. Pick a half-acre of your poor land and plant it to adapted legumes and grasses. If it is not fenced, place a good protective covering of brush over the seeding and watch the new vegetation take over and thrive. The result will encourage you to start a bigger grass improvement program.

The use of tame grass crops and legumes has done wonders in increasing the productive capacity of my cropland. I have found that nature has the profound gift of self-replenishment if given an opportunity, and this has been provided to the utmost.

Once, following a dust storm that dropped a film of silt over the ranch and near-by country, I swept up and weighed the material from a measured area on my porches at Dallas and Flat Top. The figures showed that this one dust storm, which had brought topsoil from 1,000 to 1,500 miles away, had probably dropped five hundred pounds of soil per acre on our land. Soil that leaves a farm and ranch and gets blown into the atmosphere is generally high in organic matter and available phosphorous. This new soil gets trapped in a grass cover and does not blow or wash away at Flat Top. Rains carry it into the matrix of soil and humus, where it becomes a permanent part of the ranch. On ranches where there is not enough grass cover to trap it, this new soil washes away with the first heavy rain.

Small amounts of readily available nitrate, processed by lightning in the atmosphere, are carried to earth each year by raindrops. This nitrogen is caught in a good grass cover, but is carried into gullies and creeks on land without protection. It stays on the Flat Top.

When I was first developing Flat Top, a lot of feed was bought outside the ranch. An annual amount equal to two hundred pounds of feed per acre of the ranch was bought in those days. At present considerable outside feed is purchased, largely cottonseed cake, corn, maize, and small grain.

Pasture and hay production from eight hundred acres of good farmland played an important role in hurrying the recovery of the native ranges. These high-producing tame pastures grazed a lot of animals in spring and summer so range grasses could mend and increase.

Years ago, when it cost only $8.00 to harvest a ton of Johnsongrass hay, I used to buy a neighbor's hay for $10.00

a ton instead of harvesting my own. I grazed my own John-songrass and let some native range rest. I could well afford to buy my neighbor's hay for $10.00 a ton, which was $2.00 a ton more than my own would cost if put up. Each ton of my neighbor's hay had over $2.00 worth of soil nutrients which I added to my ranch.

In 1950, Mack McConnell, of the Soil Conservation Service, gave me some facts that tell a surprising story about the fertilizing value of feeds brought in from the outside and fed on the ranch. Mack's interesting statement is quoted below:

The fertilizing constituents in manure come entirely from the feed consumed by animals. In buying and selling feeds, far too few farmers and ranchers consider their fertilizer value as well as their feeding value.

The following information is based on the average manurial values of the various feeds listed. This has been figured on the assumption that when proper care is taken of the manure, there can be recovered in the manure about 70 per cent of the phosphorous and potassium and 50 per cent of the nitrogen. The data is based on the present prices of commercial fertilizer for the factors N–P–K (nitrogen, phosphorous, and potassium).

FEEDS FED ON FLAT TOP RANCH AND THEIR MANURIAL VALUES

Kind of Feed	Amount of Feed in Tons	Manurial Value Per Ton	Total Manurial Value
Alfalfa	600	$ 4.62	$2,772.00
Johnsongrass hay	100	2.50	250.00
Linseed meal	100	8.63	863.00
Cottonseed cake	50	10.51	525.50
Wheat bran	100	5.93	593.00

Corn	-	100	2.34	234.00
Oats		75	5.46	409.50
TOTALS		1,125		$5,647.00

There is one sure-fire way to manage grass right: watch both the grass and the cattle all the time. When grass has been used enough, it is time to move the cattle to another pasture or cut down on the size of the herd before the grass is grazed too closely. I don't believe anyone can figure out a canned grazing system that tells beforehand how many cattle can safely be grazed in pastures. Nor can anyone predict which pastures should be grazed in sequence from year to year.

Good grass management calls for the exercise of horse sense, cow sense, and grass sense. A man who learns how can look at his grass at any time of the year and know whether grazing has been too heavy, too light, or just right. Knowing these things will do more to keep you in the grass and ranching business than anything else.

Long ago I learned that a cow is smart enough to balance her own diet if she has plenty of range from which to select a balanced diet. When I was a boy, cattle grazing the unfenced ranges were free to choose the kind of plants that met their nutritional needs during most of the year. Now that ranges are fenced and the free movement of the cow is limited, it becomes the manager's main job to see to it that the cow has plenty of high-quality forage to eat all year. And when the range is deficient, it is the manager's job to supplement the range feed properly in order to maintain cattle production at a high level.

There is no pat formula that will work year in and year out, because differences in rainfall from one year to the next may cut grass yield in half. Likewise, there is no one permanent stocking rate for a ranch. On Flat Top we have found that we must constantly adjust our herd numbers in line with our grass production. Understocking pays off, and if you will keep more grass than livestock, your range will get better each year. Mine has. Today it is producing several times more than it did when I bought it.

I would not attempt to write this statement if I had not had a gainful experience that I want to share. Observing the improvement of my land by my own efforts gives me more satisfaction than anything I have ever done. To take a piece of land that was not growing anything of value and then, one to three years later, have it growing good crops and grass gives a feeling of fulfillment that is richly rewarding.

I have owned Flat Top for nineteen years. If you could have seen it when I bought it and could see it now, the difference would amaze you. My grass is better and more productive than the grass around my ranch. My cattle are hog-fat most of the time and more grass is left on my ranch after wintering than grows on most near-by ranges.

I will guarantee that if you devote your efforts to making your ranch better, you will make more net profit and will be much happier than if you neglect or abuse your land. Much patience and solid planning are required to make a good ranch out of a poor one. Plans have to be made for the next day, for the next month, and for several years ahead. But the indirect and direct benefits from such efforts will be worth the trouble, as I have had the pleasure of knowing. Imagine my thrill in finding native grasses growing three feet high along my subirrigated creek bottoms during the droughty Augusts of 1953, 1954, and 1955. We cut three tons of bluestem hay per acre, whereas grass on neighboring ranches which had not been subirrigated was roasted.

Your gratification pyramids when you see a big area, formerly covered with brush so thick you could hardly crawl through it, where little or no grass could grow, now producing lush pasturage for fat cattle. You know you have done humanity as well as yourself a favor. Your satisfaction is deep, and you are humble without the spiteful flavor of "I told you so." Where you have made these kinds of rock-bottom changes from poor to wise land use, you have engaged in creative agriculture and are well on the road toward building a permanent ranch. A permanent ranch is one that will support the owner properly and become more fertile and productive each year.

I know that a rancher has heavy expenses while building up his grass and usually has to figure out some extra ways of making money so that ends will meet. Perhaps some of the activities that have helped me will suggest ways and means to others:

1. Subirrigated and irrigated bottom lands planted to grass and legumes have provided cash crops of hay and seed.

2. Registered Yorkshire hogs are raised for sale.

3. A good market has been developed in Dallas for balled live oak and Spanish oak trees used in landscaping. This

operation has paid for brush-clearing operations on many acres of range land.

4. Part of the ranch has been leased to a group of sportsmen for hunting and fishing.

There is a lot of Texas land in run-down condition that needs to be built up again and made productive. But as long as the small, uneconomic-sized farms exist, no real progress will ever be made.

Take country like mine where intensive farming is out of the question because soils are shallow—livestock farming is the only reliable kind of economy. A thousand-acre holding is the smallest unit that will support a family at all, and more acreage than this really is needed. Modern living conditions make it necessary for a farmer or rancher to spend more cash than formerly; for example, to buy a new automobile every few years and send his children to high school and sometimes to college. The dry-land livestock farmer can't make a unit of less than one thousand acres produce the needed income. The only man who can do it is the one who lives near a city or industrial area where he can find a job to supplement his farm income. Even this arrangement is not the slick proposition it is believed to be by those who haven't tried it.

The town man envies the country dweller his cheap rent, water, garden produce, milk, and eggs. It is always quite a shock to the newcomer to the country to learn that the costs of town and country living are quite similar. The farmer has a radio, television, and car, and he has to drive his car a lot. His wife shops in town two or three times a week and the children go to town schools in a bus. The farmer's water costs him more than it would in town. By the time he feeds his cows and cares for the milk and butter, he has saved very little over the cost of dairy products at the nearest store. Eggs and poultry are expensive to produce. Some commercial poultrymen work for little; some actually go broke.

You can generally live better in the country than in town, but there is not much difference in cost.

Thousands of undersized farms are operated only because of subsidies that keep them producing a pile-up of surplus corn, wheat, cotton, and other crops. I believe that the problem of overproduction could be solved if these small farm units were made into larger ones.

Artificially high prices placed on farm products have caused a backfire worse than the problem they were created to solve. The big farmers do not need subsidies. For example, a farmer who grows 25,000 bushels of wheat can make a good profit when his wheat sells at $1.50 a bushel. The cotton grower producing 100 bales can make plenty of money at 20 cents a pound. However, the small operator can not make enough money at these prices to support his family. Artificially floored prices cause buyers to purchase less of these high-priced commodities. We have greatly cut the use of cotton by selling it higher than do other countries. Cotton is too high to sell in competition with rayon, nylon, and other synthetics. Corn is too high to feed hogs and cattle and many livestock feeders are losing money.

Why not sell farm products on a free market ruled by supply and demand? If a subsidy is needed, give it for only the first ten bales of cotton a family produces, or the first

2,500 bushels of corn, and let the article sell at its natural price on the market.

I raise these controversial issues because solutions of them are essential before we can restore millions of acres of worn-out land. And this great land of ours is too valuable to let it waste away from continued neglect.

We only hold our land in trust for a few years while we live, and since countless others will use it after we are gone, each of us has an obligation to maintain our land and related resources in good condition for our own use and for those who will follow. The landowner, therefore, while having the legal right, does not have the moral right to destroy or permit others to destroy his land.

After all, ownership of land is very different from ownership of other property. The owner of a suit of clothes can wear it out and throw it away without affecting anyone else. The owner of an automobile can drive it until it will run no farther and then abandon it. The automobile will make an ugly spot on the landscape and will make less useful a very small bit of land. The complete use of most things can be had without especially affecting others. This is certainly not true of land. The owner of agricultural land has a moral obligation to the future generations who will depend on it for food and fiber long after he is gone. If he does not take upon himself the responsibility of leaving the land he occupies in a better and more fertile condition than when he received it, he may render to mankind, by having lived, a disservice instead of a service. Fortunately, the conservation and improvement of agricultural land also means greater production, more sustained yields, and bigger profits. A ranch, to continue to warrant the adjective "permanent," must also be profitable. Flat Top was developed to last and to be profitable. This book is the story of its development and of the satisfaction that has accompanied its continuing improvement.

Texans are notorious for their bragging. They have had much to brag about—an unmatched historical background, rich reserves of oil and gas, and a magnificent God-given heritage of soil, water, grass, timber, and wildlife. But our grandchildren, what will they have to brag about? Our oil and gas reserves are being steadily depleted, there is still far too much water being wasted, far too much soil being lost through water and wind erosion. Bragging about the Alamo, San Jacinto, and Adobe Walls will be hollow indeed if Texas land will not support the ever increasing population. The bragging rights of future generations of Texans are in jeopardy. Flat Top is a demonstration of what can be done with Texas soil, water, grass, and wildlife. If we all do our part for the land, our Southwest will again be as good as it was when our ancestors fought the Comanches and Santa Anna for it.

CHARLES PETTIT

Dallas, Texas
January 27, 1957

CONTENTS

ILLUSTRATIONS

FLAT TOP RANCH
The Story of a Grassland Venture

Chapter 1

TOWARDS A PERMANENT AGRICULTURE

Louis Bromfield

IT IS ONLY now, more than two centuries since farming really began on the North American continent, that we are beginning to get a genuine and a permanent agriculture. To be sure, in certain small and restricted areas such as the Pennsylvania Dutch country and the scattered Amish settlements, a sound and enduring and productive agriculture has long existed. Here and there throughout the nation there have always been isolated good farmers; but such areas and individuals represent only a minute fraction of 1 per cent of the agricultural and livestock areas of the nation; and it must be remembered that these peoples and individual ranchers have a special point of view toward the land; they do not look upon it as something to be mined as one might mine coal and exploit oil, nor do they ever believe, as did and do so many farmers and cattlemen, that their land owes them a living. They believe that their land is something to be held in trust to God, which will give them security and a good living during their lifetimes, so long as they care for it, and must be passed on to their children as rich and productive as they found it, or even more so.

The record of exploitation, waste, and destruction is written across the whole of the nation, and in the Southwest,

3

where the country is still new, the record is one of the worst. One sees all too often big ranches with ramshackle, jerry-built houses and sheds, obviously constructed in the beginning to last only until the land was worn out or the grazing gone and the owner could move on to new land, which long ago could be had free or a dollar an acre. One sees also imposing houses of wood, built originally by some settler with money who came and planned to remain in the Southwest for life. But these houses frequently tell their own particular melancholy story; they have gone unpainted or the termites and the weather have eaten into them. Around them the fields are in low production (hardly worth the trouble) or the once rich grazing land is overgrown with mesquite and weeds eaten, in drought weather, into the very earth itself. Neither the mesquite nor the weeds were there in the beginning; they came in only with the abuse of the land.

One still finds now and then in the Southwest an old-timer who remembers when the grass everywhere was so tall that it was difficult to find the cattle even from the back of a horse, or so tall that it came higher than the stirrup of a saddle. I have seen such grass only at Flat Top Ranch and in one or two places in the whole of the Southwest. How much more common is the weedy, dusty land with the earth showing through the weeds and the mesquite.

And sometimes one comes across a ranch on which the house is a modern palace and the cattle sheds compare well with good middle-class housing. The fence posts are steel and the barbed wire gold plated. Sometimes the grass or the crops are good, but sometimes the fields are no better than those which surround the leaning shack or the unpainted, termite-ridden wooden houses of the old-time well-off settler. These palaces rarely represent good agriculture or good cattle raising, although here and there their owners have at times made some valuable contributions; usually they are what is known as "oil ranches" and have little more to do with good agriculture and well-managed grazing land than those houses in the old once ruined agricultural South which were painted and roofed with what the natives used to refer to as "Coca-Cola money." Frequently these houses are convenient as tax "write offs" or the money poured into them is out of all relation to a sound and practical agriculture. They are doing little to solve the grave agricultural and grazing problems of the vast Southwest.

And there are the wheat lands, some owned by farmers who live on their land and some by the speculators known as "suitcase" farmers, who plant and go away to return months later and harvest the money from the buyer and from the taxpayers for the crop. It is from such land and from the worn-out grazing land that the dust storms come, blowing away the soil and carrying it high in the air as far east as the Atlantic. There are millions of acres of such land already abandoned and more acres on the way.

And in the country which has been fortunate enough to be blessed with underground artesian water, and so built many a quick fortune in vegetables and fruit, I have seen four-inch streams of precious water running day and night because no one had bothered to cap and conserve the flow. I have even seen deep gullies cut through rich land by the unchecked flow of priceless artesian water. In much of that country today wells no longer flow and now must be

pumped, and in some the water has given out altogether.
No one is quite certain where this water comes from, and
it is quite possible that it represents an accumulation over
thousands and millions of years and that it will be thousands or millions of years before it returns again.

One of the commonest sights of the great Southwest is
grazing land which once carried a steer the year round
on ten to twelve acres and now provides only poor grazing
for one steer on every thirty or forty acres. It should never
be forgotten that much of this land, both grazing and agricultural land, has been so ruined that the costs of restoring
it become economically impossible save as a tax "write off"
which, in the end, is paid for by other citizens.

Much of the Southwest has been fortunate indeed in the
vast richness in oil and minerals which God and luck left
to it, but over much of the great area the end of the oil and
the minerals is in sight and in some areas they have already
been used up. One day they will all be gone, and unless
other means of wealth and production are discovered, many
a city and town will become a ghost town, as indeed some
of them have already become. Old-timers will tell you of
towns where once the production of wheat and corn was
so great that for days it lay piled beside the railroad tracks
because the railroads were unable to move it fast enough.
Today they can take you back to the same towns and show
you empty shops and empty rotting buildings and a ghost-
haunted railway station. Not only has the town died, the
railroad companies have even pulled up the tracks for use
elsewhere or as scrap. Minerals, unfortunately, cannot be
grown; but agricultural and forest land and well-treated

water resources are eternally productive and eternally renewable; and it should never be forgotten that it is funda-
mentally our natural resources which are the very foundation of our great wealth and prosperity, of the stability of
our currency, and of a condition which even still today provides the American people with the finest diet, the greatest
abundance, and the cheapest food in the world.

And we should never forget that while our resources are
waning, our population increases steadily—seven thousand
and more new citizens every time the sun rises, more than
two hundred thousand every time you tear a page off the
calendar, more than three millions every year—a steady increase in population which is mounting rather than dimin-
ishing. The pressures for food and raw materials in the outside world grow daily more alarming. It is today these pressures which are the *real* cause of wars among peoples and
nations.

These elements, all added together, do not provide a
cheering picture, and nowhere in the nation is the picture
today darker than in the great Southwest, despite the great
show of wealth and bustle that appears almost everywhere
in the great cities, on the surface. The Great Southwest is
booming, but booms must always be paid for one way or
another at some time by someone; in the long run there is
never any such thing as a "quick buck." Someone, perhaps
a son or a granddaughter or a child unborn, will have to pay.
We are already leaving a vast burden to future generations
which will have no Eldorado to plunder as we have had.
Perhaps one day they will have to work, as most nations in
Europe and Asia work today, to buy the raw materials and

the food which we still have in abundance. Perhaps they will have to spend, as Britain does, one-third of the nation's income to buy food for the people, or do without as do India and China, where half the populations are born and die without ever having had enough to eat, even of the poorest food, for one day in their lives.

These disasters today seem far away. All of us alive today may be dead long before the first symptoms of real privation and disaster begin to appear, so perhaps none of it matters; but if one has any real morality of genuine religious feeling and faith, as so many of us keep asserting loudly, we are hypocrites, for there is no worse sin in the eyes of God than stealing the heritage of children as yet unborn.

In the first place there is, by necessity, a growing recognition of the economic factor in the success of any farmer or cattleman—that the more a farmer raises per acre the less it costs him to produce it in terms of taxes, interest, labor, seed, gasoline, and wear and tear on capital investment, and the bigger is his margin of profit. It is also being recognized that it is better and more profitable to raise one good steer on good grazing land of high carrying capacity than three or four "bologna, hatrack" cattle on pastures where they are eating the dust along with the poor weedy forage. This knowledge is mere fact, to be proven easily and simply by arithmetic. So also is the fact that a farmer who runs down the fertility of his fields or the carrying capacity of his grazing land is destroying his capital just as much as if he converted it into banknotes and burned them in the backyard. These facts lie in the background of a nationwide situation in which between one hundred and one hundred

Photograph by Charles J. Belden

Mr. Charles Pettit, the owner of Flat Top Ranch.

Weather vane and Flat Top monogram brand on top of the rock car port adjoining the ranch house.

and fifty thousand bad farmers a year are being liquidated every year by the mere force of economics.

No farmer in any nation in the world has so much help from government and from his fellow citizens as the American farmer. At no cost he has immense reservoirs of scientific and economic knowledge available to him. He has bulletins and the personal aid of the county agent and the Soil Conservation Service. He and his children have colleges everywhere and some of the finest experiment stations in the world. He benefits through his co-operatives and his children through Four-H clubs and the Future Farmer organizations. And there are privately endowed agricultural research foundations doing fine work, from which he is able to obtain information at no cost—for many crops he benefits by government price supports which are in turn paid for by his fellow citizens to the tune of hundreds of millions of dollars a year. There is really no excuse for a bad or an ignorant farmer or cattleman. There is only the fact that he chooses to be a bad farmer or livestock raiser.

Yet with all these aids and sources of knowledge and information, I sometimes think that a single, well-managed, profitable farm or cattle ranch can do as much or more good in a given community than all of these agencies and means of help. It is quite true that such a single farm, or ranch, is in itself a product of all of these aids and educational agencies because the proprietor of that single good prosperous operation has seen fit to learn and profit by them. In a way such farms act as the intermediary between the agencies and educational facilities and the average farmer or rancher by translating their information into sound and

9

practical fact and into a compact and workable pattern. And behind this lies another factor of great importance in the whole of the agricultural picture—that the average farmer or rancher is a pragmatist of the first order: He believes what he sees and he believes what works, and when he sees something working, he is convinced and converted.

In this lies the great importance of what the Soil Conservation Service and Tennessee Valley Authority have long described as the "pilot farm." Countless times throughout the nation I have seen the effects of such a farm in a given community: I have seen its influence in a valley or a county, extending continuously outward in concentric circles, and as it does so, I have seen erosion checked, and water kept where it belongs (in the ground). I have seen crop yields rise and profits increase both on dairy and beef herds. I have seen farms change in a few years from rapid decline to success. I have seen new buildings erected and old ones painted and repaired. The whole process of getting information and the knowledge of new and improved methods to the farmer is almost as complex as agriculture itself, but, as in life itself, nothing is more efficacious than the example.

Chapter 2

CHARLES PETTIT, CONSERVATION RANCHER
Louis Bromfield

I FIRST SAW Flat Top Ranch many years ago, and at first sight I was aware there was something about it which set it apart from most ranches and farms in the Southwest. Very clearly it was not a ramshackle operation, nor was it something which the owner had hired others to plan for him. It was a busy place with abandoned overgrown land being cleared and cedars and mesquite being cut down or sprayed in one of the many experiments which have taken place at Flat Top and been of value to the whole of the Southwest. It is notable that the ranch management has always been highly co-operative with research and experiment, whether with large commercial organizations or with experiment stations, foundations, and laboratories. This ranch very clearly had a direction, and the hand at the helm was an owner who took a personal interest in everything that went on. It had that atmosphere of care, planning, and accomplishment which goes only with ranches, farms, or estates which are loved by the owner.

The ranch, I discovered, was made up of about seventeen thousand acres of land lying near the small town called Walnut Springs in east central Texas between Waco and Fort Worth. It was not in the richest part of Texas. It was in cedar country and the farms which went into its making had

11

been in an abandoned or semi-abandoned condition when they were thrown together to make Flat Top. Its history was like that of much of the Southwest; within three or four generations it had nearly been farmed and grazed out of existence. One of the great advantages was the springs and a small stream called the East Fork of the Bosque which ran almost through the center of the ranch and was fed by small tributaries originating in springs in small hollows and ravines.

It is unnecessary to describe the immense value of a water supply on any farm or ranch in the Southwest. But in the beginning at Flat Top, the little river was neither so well-behaved nor so serviceable as it has long since become. Although there was always some water in the stream, there were times when portions of it went dry, and in case of heavy rain it was frequently filled with flood water and sometimes with silt that came off the shabby grazing land and down the deep gullies.

In the beginning Flat Top was no better and no worse than many a ranch or farm in the Southwest. It was, you might say, typical of far too much of that vast area. A few more years of farming and grazing such as it had known in the past and it would have reached that point where it would have been, economically speaking, hardly worth reclamation.

But Flat Top was lucky. It caught the attention and the liking of a man who had been brought up on a ranch, run a country store, and made a considerable success in life. His heart was always with the land and with livestock, and he had the intelligence and the imagination to see that out of the weedy, eroded pastures and the depleted bottom lands something could be built and something that might be very fine and very valuable. In the beginning Charlie Pettit looked on the Flat Top Project as a kind of part-time job, not by any means a hobby, but an enterprise which would occupy him as he gradually withdrew from an active business life into retirement and one in which he could very possibly make a contribution to the welfare of Texas and the whole of the Southwest. It took a great vision to see the possibilities of creating out of those mesquite and cedar pastures, gullies, and bare hilltops, the beautiful ranch today widely known as Flat Top. Once the project was undertaken it consumed more and more of the owner's time, until for the past few years the ranch has come to occupy virtually all his energy and attention.

And what of the owner of Flat Top? He is a small, wiry, and very nearly indestructible man. He has survived two or three bad automobile accidents and two or three illnesses which might have put an end to many another man. Despite all this, he has an energy and a vitality which I have seen in very few young men. He is also a naturally good man and consequently a happy one. He has been and is a successful man and he has made his own success. He has a fine family and a wonderful wife, whom he married very young when he had very little of worldly goods, who has shared his success, his friends, and his satisfaction. He has a gift for friendship and I consider him one of my best friends, which is not surprising since we share so many interests, from soils and livestock to the game of dominoes. We were brought together by agriculture and livestock in

13

the beginning, and we share a truly passionate desire to preserve and restore our land, our forest, our water resources, our wildlife and all the things which make for security and a decent life for mankind.

His whole history is intensely and typically American and even pioneer American. He was born in Michigan and moved first with his parents to Missouri and finally to Texas, where they hoped to better their fortunes in the new country. Young Charlie grew up on a ranch in Archer County (where the nearest post office was Henrietta, Texas, in Clay County), went through the schools, and had two years at the University of Texas. For some years he taught school and then went into business with a country general store which had considerable success. While in Eastland, Texas, he married a fellow school teacher, Bertie Sanders, and although the small business was doing well enough, Charlie Pettit saw in it no great future. For a time he traded successfully in land equities and finally took a flier in the oil business which turned out well. From there on his way was successful, prosperous, and solid.

But always in the background was this steady, earnest desire for land. It was in his blood as it is in the blood of so many Americans who do not realize it until they are middle-aged and find that while they have "taken the boy out of the country, they have never taken the country out of the boy." I have seen the pattern repeated again and again—that of a successful businessman or executive who tentatively buys a piece of land and finds presently that it is absorbing all his interest and sometimes a good part of his income and that, perhaps for the first time in his life, he is doing exactly what he wants to do and is thoroughly healthy, happy, and relaxed. Very frequently these men make very great contributions to agriculture and the livestock industry. They are obviously men of brains and ability, for they have made a success of life, and, very often, they bring these same talents at middle age or after to the land and to cattle breeding.

Very clearly this was what happened in the case of Flat Top and its owner. One sees the evidence on all sides in the planning and the permanence and carrying out of a definite and co-ordinated program. More and more the fact is being recognized that the business of agriculture is not merely that of growing cash crops and selling them, that raising livestock is not merely a matter of turning them loose on mediocre or poor grazing land (frequently in too great numbers) and letting nature take its course.

The great value of Flat Top Ranch and ranches and farms like it is to show what can be done and how to do it. Already the Soil Conservation Service, together with other agencies and the example of "pilot farms," has accomplished a near miracle; in the short space of a few years the whole psychology of the nation has been changed, and it is no longer possible to find a really intelligent farmer who would challenge the established principles of the conservation of soil and water. This, of course, has been an immense step forward in American agriculture, but—and this is a very big *but*—we should never overlook the fact that in all this change the force of economics has played a great role. In a country where there is no more free good land to be had for the taking and where population pressures are on the increase, agriculture is beginning to approach a maturity in which there is no longer a place for the bad or the greedy farmer; the land, the equipment, the buildings, and the livestock cost too much. Economics in the end will take care of the bad farmer despite price supports, subsidies, or what you will; economics will simply eliminate him.

Money has gone into the making of Flat Top as it indeed must go into any sound and progressive enterprise anywhere—money which, as in many similar ventures, has come originally from other enterprises; but how, indeed, does one get started in farming and ranching today without capital? The simple answer is that one does not get started.

Among many city people even today there is a kind of childish idea that if a man wants to start farming, all he has to do is to start farming. And among farmers, sometimes good ones who have inherited nearly everything they possess and should know better, I have heard occasional sneers at the men who made their money elsewhere and invested it in farms. Where would some of these farmers be today if their land, and very often their livestock, their machinery, and the house they live in, had not been left them without any capital investment whatever on their part? A great many of them would certainly not be in the farming or ranching business today.

The fact is that few things today are more difficult than for a young man to get started on his own as a farmer. Scores of young men and young couples come to Malabar Farm each year to ask, "How can we get a start at farming with little or no capital?" The only honest answer I can give them is a short and harsh one, simply, "You can't." For a young man to get started today on even a small farm of average fertility within decent range of markets, a capital of forty to fifty thousand dollars is needed to purchase the land, the machinery, and the livestock necessary to a profitable operation. Not so long ago, one could have said to such a young man, "Borrow the money to buy yourself a team, a plow, and a harrow, and the government will give you rich virgin land for nothing." But those days are past.

Capital went into Flat Top Ranch and money has gone into improving and restoring it, but the investment in a practical sense has been a good one, if on no other basis than that of a gain in capital values, for the ranch today, like many another restored farm or ranch in the nation, is worth many times the price paid for it. This capital-increase factor is much more important in the whole business of restoring poorly treated land than has been understood or realized. Flat Top, like many another similar one, is a profitable investment.

In developing the ranch, Charlie Pettit has come to realize also, as has many a shrewd and practiced agricultural economist, that in areas where, like much of the Southwest, there are great stretches of marginal land, the climate is violent at times, and the country is subject to periodic droughts, land holdings that are too small can only lead in the end to bankruptcy and ruin. You cannot make of marginal cropland small, rich, and highly productive farms. In the rich Middle West with its excellent soil and good climatic conditions, a well-managed farm of 120 acres may provide a family with a good living and prosperity, and send the children to college, but throughout the Southwest there is little land where a farm as small as 120 acres will not lead sooner or later to bankruptcy and starvation. The plight of the "Okies" immortalized by Steinbeck in *The Grapes of Wrath* was not caused by the shiftlessness of the individual farmer or the harsh behavior of banks and land corporations; it was caused by the ruinous policy of the government in restricting homesteading of federal lands to a quarter-section to the individual. Most of the land opened for settlement was in reality grazing and cattle land. In addition, the vagaries of a climate where floods and droughts frequently alternated made farming a hazardous affair indeed. In order to make a living (which was not possible from grazing on 160 acres), most of these settlers raised cash crops and the climate quickly did the rest, and much of the land threatened to become desert until it was turned back into larger holdings of grazing land.

Perhaps the most interesting single factor at Flat Top Ranch is the breadth of the program which has a sound and broad ecological base. "Ecology" and "The Ecology of Man" sounds like a sixty-four-dollar word, but its meaning is really quite simple; it is concerned with how man can best live in relation to his natural surroundings, in terms of economics, of nutrition and health, of recreation, and of over-all general welfare. It is interesting to witness the rapid spread of this conception of farming and ranching throughout the nation. One sees it in the advance of soil and water conservation practices, the building of farm ponds, the care of forests and woodlots, the creation of conditions which favor wildlife, and a hundred other ways. Only in limited and backward or single-cash-crop areas has this whole conception of agriculture, long established in older countries, failed to make much headway, and such areas, based always upon a speculative crop, with all the eggs in one basket, are always certain to be backward in most of the broader aspects not only of agriculture but of living.

This broad ecological base and conception are abundantly evident at Flat Top. First of all come the buildings, which are constructed largely of stone, and well constructed on a *permanent* basis. One does not have the impression, drawn from cheap and untidy shacks, that this is merely a fly-by-night operation. The buildings at Flat Top are here to stay; they were built by a man who did not look upon agriculture and grazing land as something to be mined and exploited. He regarded them as permanent investments and the money put into them a sound capital investment. They are a symbol of an agriculture and a grazing program that are here to stay.

Not the least important aspect of the program is that of proper land use, which is the basis of any sound agriculture. Those fields which are obviously made for grazing because the soils are shallow and unsuited, especially in dry, hot weather, for raising crops, are left to grazing, but grazing which includes rest periods for the turf to establish itself, seeding of worn-out cultivated land, clearing of mesquite and cedar, and controlling those broadleafed weeds which rob the grass and legumes of moisture in the early spring.

The land which is not strictly grazing land is sometimes used for crops, but the main burden of the crop-growing is placed upon the flatter land and the bottom land where irrigation is possible as a guarantee against the long, terrible droughts which frequently occur in the Southwest. In these areas the land is properly treated as the high-grade land it is, by maintaining and even greatly increasing its natural fertility.

But irrigation cannot be practiced efficiently and profitably where there are insufficient reserves of water, and in the beginning there was insufficient water at Flat Top. This occasional shortage of irrigation water has been wholly corrected by one of the finest programs for the conservation of water I have seen anywhere in the United States. Bit by bit, with the ranch's own equipment, there has been constructed a whole big chain of ponds and lakes which provide ample water for cattle and for intensive irrigation. Not only do these ponds and lakes fill naturally in time from the waters of the East Bosque, but they capture the immense amounts of water which come in the form of violent and heavy rains that are at once the blessing and the curse of the Southwest—the blessing because water there is always needed and the curse because all too frequently they come in torrential downpours which run off the land carrying topsoil with them and are wasted. Virtually all of this water is conserved in the small ponds and the lakes at Flat Top, and in turn these reservoirs are so skillfully planned and constructed that in case the water in one of them becomes exhausted during a long drought, water from a pond above may be transferred merely by gravity.

And beyond all this lies the program for wildlife which contributes so much to the general welfare of the ranch and the recreation of the workers on it and their friends.

Charles Pettit, Conservation Rancher

The ponds and lakes used to store irrigation water have been stocked with bass, bream, and other game fish which propagate to a point where fishing becomes a duty in order to reduce the excess population. There is an abundance of quail, both of the bobwhite and blue varieties, because considerable areas of land in the ravines and steep ridges near the streams and lakes have been left in thick cover which also provides shelter for great numbers of wild turkeys. The deer population has long since become a problem both through breeding and because the deer are naturally attracted to Flat Top from throughout the whole surrounding area by the superior grazing and forage and water supplies available there. There is even a small herd of antelope, one of the prettiest of animals.

The Hereford cattle raised on the ranch are known everywhere in the world, and at Flat Top they live and breed in the very best of natural conditions with as little as possible that is artificial in their surroundings.

I recognize the great contributions Charlie Pettit has made through breeding to the cattle industry, but I confess I have been most interested in the reclamation, conservation, and maintenance of the land at Flat Top; in the restoring of old worn-out grazing and agricultural areas; and in the experimentation in new grasses and legumes and their proper use and development. Charlie Pettit has been a pioneer in helping to establish a permanent agriculture and cattle operation in the Southwest. This permanent approach to agriculture and grazing activities is something which the nation as a whole must learn to practice if our welfare and prosperity is to be maintained. Charlie Pettit

21

is doing his part in showing the way—he is a good citizen and I can't think of higher praise than that.

I know of no spot in the world I would rather visit than Flat Top, for here lies accomplishment, here lie objectives and ideals, here is food as good as I have ever eaten in the best restaurants and the greatest houses of London, Paris, or New York. In the evening when I am staying at Flat Top, Charlie Pettit and I sometimes drive out to watch the wild-life before the sun goes down. The handsome Herefords lift their faces and stare at us peacefully as we drive past. On the lakes and ponds in the spring and autumn there are always whole fleets of wild ducks and geese. In the dusk, if you watch carefully, you can see the big wild turkey gob-blers making their way up to the very tops of the pecan trees to roost for the night, or perhaps a turkey hen followed by a dozen young poults scuttering into the underbrush. And there are always deer starting up the slopes and stopping at a distance to watch you, and in the evening light the white tails of the antelope stand out like beacons. Here in the midst of what in 1955 was a four-year drought there is good grazing on the fields; there is water everywhere and the bottom fields are green with alfalfa and grain crops. Like every good ranch, Flat Top is a small world in itself, where every law of the universe is in constant operation. As the evening closes in and we drive back to the big, simple, and comfortable ranch house to the best of suppers, pro-duced out of the land itself, I know that I am riding beside a happy man who has built, and indeed created, something fine which not only brings him pleasure but is of great bene-fit to his fellow man. How far removed he is from the parasite and the speculator, and how well he knows how to spend his money, which is one of the most difficult things in the world to do.

The lights come on in the distant ranch house and I know that what I have been seeing and what has been done here all about me is founded upon the most important of all human goals and is the very foundation of human decency—something which Albert Schweitzer, one of the great men of our times, has described as "Reverence for Life."

Chapter 3

GEOLOGY AND SOILS
Charles Clinton Booth

FLAT TOP IS an ancient grazing ground where a variety of prehistoric animals have grazed at different geologic periods. At times the area was under the sea and at times it was dry land. At one ancient time dinosaurs grazed the area, and during the Ice Age, primeval elephants, bison, horses, camels, and pigs lived in the country.

The geologic history of the area near Flat Top Ranch is characterized by the deposition of several thousand feet of sedimentary rock on top of Pre-Cambrian granite. There are about 7,200 feet of Paleozoic strata overlain by a few hundred feet of Cretaceous age strata. The rocks which outcrop on Flat Top Ranch are the Fredericksburg group, Lower Cretaceous in age.

The oldest and lowest formation is the Paluxy sandstone. The Paluxy is about fifty to sixty feet thick and consists of fine-grained, quite porous, compact yet unindurated sand, generally white with lenses and patches of yellow, red, and brown. The sand is crossbedded and the cement is generally calcareous, with a greater percentage toward the top of the formation. There are pieces of fossilized and charred wood in the Paluxy sandstone and several good dinosaur tracks and ripple marks in a limestone stringer on the bottom of Rough Creek in the northeastern part of the ranch. The

24

Bluestem seed hay spread on ground prepared for seeding protects the soil from erosion and shades tender seedlings until they are established.

Flat Top land on the left side of the fence is striking evidence of the results obtained from cedar eradication and moderate use of grass.

Flat Top Mountain, the ranch's place name, in a setting of bluestem grass.

Back-up water behind a dam flooding one of the narrow valleys along the East Bosque.

Paluxy sands were laid down in rather shallow marine waters near the shore.

The Walnut marl overlies the Paluxy sandstone and is about ninety feet thick in this area. It is made up of alternating beds of limestone; marl and shell masses. The Walnut contains abundant pelecypods (oysters) of several varieties, and was probably laid down under near shore marine conditions.

The Comanche Peak limestone overlies the Walnut marl and has a thickness of about eighty feet in this area. It is a chalky, nodular, cream-white limestone with a few medium bedded limestone beds toward the top. This formation was laid down under near shore marine conditions and contains abundant gastropods (snails), oysters, and ammonites.

The Edwards limestone overlies the Comanche Peak limestone, and is a hard, massive, porous, non-dolomitic, tan, reef limestone with splotches of replacement pyrite. This offshore marine reef is composed of many fossils and fossil fragments, as it was chiefly organic at the time of its deposition. This formation is about twenty-five feet thick.

The Kiamichi is the highest and youngest formation exposed on Flat Top Ranch. It is composed of shaly marl, succeeded by interbedded limestone and marl. This formation is offshore marine and contains some snails, oysters, and ammonites.

Flat Top Ranch is between the western Cross Timbers and the eastern Cross Timbers, and is in the Lampasas Cut Plain of the Comanche Plateau. This plateau slopes east with approximately the same dip as the limestone beds of the Comanchean Series.

The area is within the Brazos River drainage; it is drained to the south by Flag Branch, East Bosque Creek, Rough Creek, and Mustang Creek, all of which flow into the Bosque River, which in turn empties into the Brazos River at Waco. These streams are intermittent and retained only a few holes of water during dry weather before dams were constructed. This area is on a drainage divide between the Brazos River and one of its largest tributaries, the Bosque River. Consequently, Fredericksburg strata are present on the inter-drainage divide.

The soils of Flat Top Ranch are related directly to the rock type of the underlying formation. The soil types are classified by Bushnell (1923) as: Frio silty clay loam, colluvial phase; San Saba clay; Trinity clay; Denton clay; Denton stony clay; Bracket gravelly loam; and Windthorst, colluvial phase.

Frio silty clay loam, colluvial phase, consists of a brown to dark brown friable silty clay loam passing into brown silty clay loam. This soil is found in the larger creek beds, which derive their water from the higher limestone and marl formations.

San Saba clay consists of black heavy clay underlain by dark brown clay and then, not deeper than two feet, underlain by soft, white limy material. This soil overlies the upper Walnut, the Comanche Peak, the Edwards, and the Kiamichi formations.

Trinity clay consists of very dark brown to black clay underlain by dark brown, dark ashy gray, grayish brown, or yellowish brown calcareous clay. This soil is found in the stream valleys subject to overflow.

Geology and Soils

The Denton clay is a brown to dark brown clay passing into lighter clay and then into yellowish brown friable clay, grading into a larger percentage of limy material at greater depths. The soil is usually about three feet thick. This soil is formed at some localities on the upper Walnut marl and the Comanche Peak limestone.

Denton stony clay consists of dark brown clay underlain by grayish or yellowish brown, friable, calcareous clay resting on the marl or limestone. This soil is usually about fifteen inches thick and, like the Denton clay, is underlain by the upper Walnut marl and the Comanche Peak limestone.

Bracket gravelly loam is a light gray, grayish brown, or brownish gray, friable, gravelly loam or gravelly clay loam underlain by a cream-colored gravelly, marly clay. The subsoil has a faint pinkish color at some localities. The Bracket gravelly loam is underlain by the Comanche Peak limestone.

There is a small amount of Windthorst fine sandy loam, colluvial phase, in this area. Windthorst fine sandy loam is found on the land subject to overflow by Rough Creek and the East Bosque Creek.

The use of the land for agriculture is controlled by the soils, which are in turn controlled by the underlying formations. The best land under cultivation consists of alluvial deposits adjacent to the streams. There is also some cultivated land in the soils overlying the Paluxy sandstone and the Walnut marl, particularly where the Walnut is very marly. On top of one range of hills, the lower Kiamichi, or the marly and shaly part, is cultivated. The rest of the area supports prairie, trees, and brush, depending on the amount of clearing done.

There are two water sources in the area: wells and rain. The wells are adequate to satisfy the needs of humans and animals, but it is not economical to irrigate large areas from them. The wells produce water from the Paluxy and several zones in the Trinity. The Paluxy water is excellent in quality but limited in quantity. There is considerable Trinity water, but it is less desirable because of its mineral content.

The prominent topographical feature for which the ranch was named, Flat Top Mountain, is situated near the southern edge of the ranch. This hill has an elevation of about 1,250 feet and stands above the surrounding valley by about two hundred feet. The top twenty-five feet of this feature is made up of the Edwards reef limestone. This formation is rather hard and resistant to erosion, and is partially responsible for the presence of Flat Top Mountain, as well as the other flat-topped hills in this area. The underlying eighty feet is Comanche Peak limestone. It is rather easily eroded and forms rather steep sides under the Edwards cap. Below the Comanche Peak limestone and forming the base of the hill is the Walnut marl which contains some resistant beds and accounts for the undulating topography surrounding the mountain.[1]

[1] REFERENCES: T. M. Bushnell, "Soil survey of Erath County, Texas," U.S. Department of Agriculture, Bureau of Soils, 1923; Charles Clinton Booth, "Geology of Chalk Mountain Quadrangle, Bosque, Erath, Hamilton and Somervell Counties, Texas," M.A. Thesis, University of Texas, 1956.

Chapter 4

GRASSLAND IMPROVEMENT AND CONSERVATION

B. W. ALLRED

CIVILIZATION HAS INVADED and killed out millions of acres of bluestem sod that once produced an ocean of waving grass in the great American heartland. But there are a few ranches with some of it left, and it is paying its way to stockmen who own it.

The Flat Top is one of the few spreads where big bluestem, little bluestem, Indiangrass, and switchgrass grow tall enough in valleys to hide a bunch of Herefords. Even on the upland prairies the bluestems and sideoats grama grow high enough to brush away the flies from cows' bellies as they wade through the grass, picking a living.

What is being done to improve this range has deep meaning to owners in the large bluestem belt because many are following this example, and this means better grass and greater security for farmers and ranchmen.

The bluestem belt, the most productive native grassland of the primeval American continent, lay in the area extending from Lake Winnipeg, Canada, to the Gulf of Mexico. It was bounded on the east by the hardwood forest and on the west by the Great Plains. This rich area has been changed more than any other American grassland as a result of settlement, farming, grazing, and burning.

The ranch headquarters is five miles northwest of Walnut Springs, Texas. Most of the ranch lies in Bosque County with small acreages in Somervell and Erath counties. Its geographical position is between the 97 and 98 meridians and slightly above north latitude 32.

A number of events that have made interesting Texas history occurred on and near the Flat Top. Cabeza de Vaca and the Negro, Esteban, were the first Europeans known to have entered the bluestem belt. Some authorities believe they came nearly as far north as Flat Top. These two unfortunates were the only survivors of a Spanish exploratory fleet shipwrecked near the mouth of the Sabine River in 1528. They wandered for several years over the bluestem prairies of South Texas as captives and slaves of various Indian tribes.

Finally, after several years of peril and hardships, they ran into some Spaniards near Culicán, Mexico, and returned to civilization. The extravagant tales told about the seven golden cities of Cíbola, by Esteban, excited the gold-hungry Spaniards. After hearing these tales, Coronado organized his famous fortune-hunting expedition to find Cíbola, and false-hearted Indian guides led them on a fruitless chase as far north as Kansas.

The ranch lies near the western edge of the famous Eastern Cattle Trail, over which nearly four million Longhorn cattle were trailed to northern markets. The Texas Longhorn originated in Mexico from descendants of the first cattle introduced into Mexico in 1521 by Gregario de Villalobos. The foundation Texas cattle, two hundred head, were trailed from Mexico across the southern end of the bluestem belt and delivered to a Spanish mission on the Texas and Louisiana line in 1690.

Spanish cattle multiplied and ran wild along the Gulf Coast. These old "Corrientes" mothered the Texas Longhorn breed in the tall bluestem grasses of the prairies between the Trinity and Nueces rivers.

There was no outlet for the surplus cattle that loaded the ranges during the Civil War. Cattle were thin, and the bluestem was grubbed to the nub. Then the relief lines, the cattle trails to Kansas railheads and Montana and Dakota miners and Indian agencies, opened up.

The Eastern Trail ran north and south through the bluestem belt. That part of the trail extending through part of the Indian Territory, now Oklahoma, was called the Chisholm Trail. The Eastern Trail began near Kingsville, Texas, and joined the Chisholm Trail north of the Red River crossing, near Bowie, Texas. Cattle off the Texas bluestem ranges drained in from feeder trails below the Red River and followed the Chisholm Trail to Kansas, where some were shipped eastward by rail. Others were dispersed northward over forking trails leading to various destinations.

Many herds were delivered to railheads and Indian agencies as beeves, and northern ranchers preferred to buy fat cattle that would winter well; consequently the trail drivers spread the herds through the best grass in order to fatten them on the way. As much as possible, the trail bosses kept their cattle away from heavily grazed areas except as they were forced to concentrate for safe crossings on rivers or for water. At places the trails were fifty miles wide, representing a broad lane rather than a narrow trail. Flat Top

lay in the path of one of the feeder trails that joined the
Eastern Trail near Fort Worth. It grazed its share of Longhorn cattle in those golden days.

Flat Top is grassy and is getting grassier under the Pettit
system of grassland ranching which has performed an apparent miracle of resurrection on land which had been
eroded and damaged for many years. Serious washing has
been stopped, with grass now healing gullies. Not an acre
of soil blows on Flat Top even when winds are whirling
white-colored sand geysers skyward from bare peanut
fields a few miles away in the Cross Timbers. Flat Top
cattle winter strongly and remain in fine condition even
in late winter. Even the sharp rocks on the hillsides are
cushioned with the felted residues of left-over grass at the
end of the grazing season.

When Charlie Pettit put together several miscellaneous
holdings into the present ranch, he inherited a maze of
problems. For example, a lot of the grassland had deteriorated to poor condition, some was in fair condition, very
little was in good condition, and only a few areas a long
way from waterings were in excellent condition. Weedy
forbs and low-grade grasses were far more plentiful than
the top-grade bluestems, Indiangrass, switchgrass, and sideoats grama that now thrive on the ranch.

Twenty-five per cent of the land was covered with suffo-
cating stands of trees and brush. In 1860, the upland prairies
had been free of trees and brush because bluestem had been
king and was in control. At that time the stream valleys
had open stands of pecan, several kinds of oak, elms, and
other trees growing in tall grass. On slopes leading out of

valleys were scattered trees of live oak, Spanish oak, and cedar elm, forming open savannah with the bluestem grasses. Scattered and stunted shinnery oak grew harmoniously with grass on the rocky butte tips. There was no cedar. The subsequent overdrain on grass by the livestock following settlement reduced the grass stands, and then the trees suckered and thickened; cedar, shrubs, and vines invaded and converted the stream valleys into impenetrable thickets. Tree and brush stands thickened on slopes and hilltops until grasses could not grow. Sun-loving grasses couldn't thrive in the shade and grazing capacity was reduced to practically nothing.

Twenty-five per cent of the land was covered by a scrub forest that had little commercial value. Yet the ranchers who pioneered before the days of barbed wire found too little suitable timber for fence building and were forced to use rock for fencing material.

On the land that is now Flat Top Ranch there were 3,400 acres that had been cropped, but only 1,000 was suitable for cropping. Twenty-four hundred acres needed to be planted to grass and much of it was badly eroded, infertile, and caked as hard as flint. Suitable native grass seed was not available.

But today Flat Top is over the hump. The native bluestem ranges have improved. A range survey made in 1950, a year before a bad drought, by Clyde Wells and Arthur Bell, Soil Conservation Service range men working with the Bosque Soil Conservation District, shows that most of the ranges have improved to fair and good condition; many have progressed to excellent condition, and very few spots are in poor condition. A current recheck shows that the ranges not only held their own during five years of drought but many pastures continued to improve, as indicated by the abundance of seedling grasses of several better kinds. Buffalograss, a short grower, is about the only one that lost ground during the drought.

The heavy end of the brush and tree clearing jobs has been accomplished and a little finishing here and there plus yearly maintenance work is all that remains to be done.

About 2,400 acres of abandoned cropland has been successfully regrassed and most of these new pastures are furnishing grazing for cattle.

Almost 1,000 acres of good productive crop land are used to grow pasture and supplemental feed for the cattle. The important forage crops are alfalfa, oats, barley, button clover, Madrid sweetclover, sudan, and Johnsongrass.

The grass story on the Flat Top was summed up aptly by a visitor in 1954. Bill Roberts, ranch manager, took him on an extensive trip over the pastures and finally at one of the stops to look around, the tourist wryly said, "I tell you, grass is going to take the place."

Charlie Pettit is a conservation rancher who has achieved conservation while using his soil, water, and vegetation correctly and profitably. But in his own words, he says: "If a ranching enterprise is permanent, productivity and fertility of the land will increase and a profit will be realized."

The Flat Top staff have maintained open and alert minds for ideas and methods that reduce risk and gamble and assure success in all jobs done. About every new science that can be applied profitably has been used to the utmost on grazing, farming, and livestock programs.

The Flat Top owner has always been a fanatic about stopping water losses and improving grass and soil fertility. Some time after he started his ranch improvement program, he arranged to have a range and soil survey made by Soil Conservation Service technicians from the Bosque Soil Conservation District. The survey yielded some basic information valuable in sizing up future land-improvement and conservation needs.

Most of the soils are heavy textured and about 1,800 acres are deep and fertile, suitable for cropping. These soils are the most productive grassland soils too, as their great depth gives them water-holding capacity that is superior and extra runoff and fertility drains onto them from adjoining lands.

The important native grasses for this site are big bluestem, little bluestem, Indiangrass, switchgrass, and Canada and Virginia wildrye. Where trees furnish summer shade, cool-season grasses predominate, the most common being Canada and Virginia wildrye and Texas wintergrass.

Two other range sites make up the bulk of the ranch land; one has soil of medium depth; soil on the other is shallow. Neither site is suitable for farming.

Productivity and fertility of the soils of the site of medium depth are considerably less than those of the deep site. Important grasses are big and little bluestem, switchgrass, Indiangrass, with sideoats grama, Texas wintergrass, and the hairy form of tall dropseed in minority.

35

Soils of the shallow site are the least fertile on the ranch, but will produce thrifty stands of grass. The important grasses on the shallow site are little bluestem, sideoats grama, hairy grama, tall grama, hairy dropseed, Texas wintergrass, and Indiangrass.

There are about five thousand different kinds of flowering plants in Texas and over five hundred of these are grasses. The Flat Top Ranch has eighty-eight known grasses and several hundred other plants, many of which are valuable for grazing at some seasons of the year. While some ten or twelve grasses already named make up the bulk of the diet for the Flat Top herd, there are several hundred plants that provide some forage during the year as the animals graze cafeteria style and pick according to seasonal preference from the many available.

The native plants of the prairie have survived thousands of years of rugged natural selection and are conditioned to the rigors of fluctuating climate. These plants have survived under grazing pressures imposed on them by native American grazing animals such as buffalo and deer; hence they are not pampered garden pets.

Although their nutrient content fluctuates greatly from green to dormant state, the forage value of the native vegetation averages quite high for the year. Chemical analyses, made by the United States Soil Conservation Service, of Texas plants, many of them from or near the Flat Top Ranch, reveal their protein content, an indispensable food high in minerals and vitamins that are so necessary for growth, reproduction, and muscle building. The average protein content of grasses in all stages of growth was 9.43

per cent; for native legumes it was 19.07 per cent; for forbs 14.79 per cent; and for leaves of trees and shrubs 14.98 per cent. The average protein content of these forages is above the minimum requirements for animals. However, most of these plants are too low in protein during the dormant state to meet the body requirements of animals; hence protein supplements must be fed at such times.

The grasses supply the bulk of the animals' diet, but other plants provide variety. There are several legumes, numerous other forbs, and leaves of some trees and shrubs that are highly nutritious for short periods and add much quality to animals' diet.

For example, the ranch has excellent native legumes, such as groundplum milkvetch, catclaw sensitivebriar, and Illinois bundleflower, that are as deep rooted and nutritious as alfalfa. There are many deep-rooted nutritious perennial non-grassy herbs or forbs growing harmoniously with the bluestems when ranges are in good to excellent condition. Maximilian sunflower, Engelmanndaisy, compassplant, dotted gayfeather, and prairie parsley are examples of some of these excellent forbs.

Oak leaves are relished by animals in the spring, and leaves of the evergreen live oak provide green forage to animals in winter, a time when most grasses and forbs are dormant and low in carotene and protein. Jerseytea is a small palatable shrub that is increasing on the shallow sites since sound grazing management has been introduced.

There are few poisonous plants on the ranch. There are scattered stands of larkspur and loco, and of course young oak leaves are poisonous when they emerge in the spring.

However, losses from plant poisoning are unknown on Flat Top because animals have so much to eat all year that they never are forced to eat enough poisonous plants to hurt them.

Fleshing of the herd gives the best answer to the question of feeding quality of the native grasses. Flat Top cattle are fat all year, even cows nursing calves. Most of the cattle pick their living from the ranges all year. From November to March, since the protein is low in the bluestems and other warm-season grasses, cows and calves are given one and one-half pounds of protein daily and dry cattle get one pound. Hay is fed only during stormy weather.

Cattle find considerable green grazing in winter from a wide-leaf sedge, succulent leafy rosettes of forbs like the Engelmanndaisy as well as the leaves of Texas wintergrass, the wildryes, rescuegrass, and tall dropseed.

Part of the herd gets some winter green grazing in tame pastures of small grain, rescuegrass, button clover, Madrid sweetclover, and alfalfa.

Too many ranches are hand-to-mouth operations, where animals get too little winter grazing and mature cattle usually lose from eighty to two hundred pounds from winter starvation. But not on the Flat Top. Here cattle weights do not fluctuate greatly from winter to summer because there is always more feed than they can eat. Manager Bill Roberts says that many visitors are awed that the cattle don't get the creeps from eating bluestem. Bill does not cotton to the old tale that bluestem makes cattle creepy. Flat Top cattle eat more bluestem than cattle get on most ranches, and Bill says they have never had a creepy cow on the spread.

38

Grassland Improvement and Conservation

"Have More Feed than You Need" is a motto the ranch has adopted to keep the grass coming, the cattle fat, and the costs at a minimum. Lenient use of grass, with occasional rests for pastures when they need it, has been found to be the cheapest way to improve the condition of rundown ranges. This method gives the grasses a chance to make seed and to spread from buds and rootstocks.

Many of the former abandoned croplands were self-seeded from adjoining well-managed range lands. Native grass seed produced on the ranch was used to plant about 1,200 acres of former cropland. Most of the seed was sown with a drill, and some grass was cut as hay with mature seed and scattered with a manure spreader. This hay-method of seeding is particularly good where soils are infertile and tend to seal over and crust. New seedlings are not grazed until the second or third year after planting as this gives new plants their chance to get a strong foothold.

Most of the remaining range planting was completed during the winter and spring of 1956. Seed from the mid and tall native grasses was used. Five hundred acres of poorly grassed, rocky, chalky ridges and steep slopes were planted to home-raised sideoats grama seed. Men walked and scattered the seed by hand. Seeding rate was four pounds per acre. Such stony lands make satisfactory seedbeds without preparation as seed lodges amongst rocks and pebbles where it germinates in the protective shallow rock mulch.

A firm seed bed was prepared in the fall of 1955 on forty-five acres of former cropland in the northeast pasture. In March of 1956, this land was planted to native tall grass seed harvested on the ranch. This field benefits from seep-

39

age during the spring of the year, which makes it a particularly favorable growing place for the native tall grasses which thrive under such conditions.

Along the creek bottoms are sundry fields formerly rescued from weedy trees and shrubs that have been planted to improved strains of big bluestem, sideoats grama, and switchgrass. These were planted in thirty-six-inch rows and will be cultivated and irrigated for seed production. These fields were in alfalfa, Madrid sweetclover, or Austrian winter peas from one to three years before grass was planted. Fields were prepared for seeding in the fall of 1955.

Thirty-five acres of the Kaw strain of big bluestem were planted along East Bosque creek. Another thirty acres were sown to sideoats grama along East Bosque creek and Flag Branch. Also eight acres of Blackwell switchgrass and fifty acres of Caddo switchgrass seed were drilled in the bottom land near the bull barn.

Nineteen acres more of big bluestem and ten acres of Indiangrass were planted along other cleared areas along East Bosque. Another forty acres of native bluestem mixture were seeded in the east central part of the ranch.

James E. Smith, Soil Conservation Service plant materials technician, served as adviser on this new grass-seeding work. The first weed crop was killed late in March by shallow tilling with a one-way plow. Broadleafed weeds in grass rows were killed with a 2,4-D hormone spray; later, Johnsongrass competition was mowed to give young tall grass seedlings a better chance to grow.

Planting of the irrigated acreage was delayed until late

A properly girdled corky tree. The 2,4,5-T spray comes into contact with the cambium zone all the way around, where it is absorbed, causing the tree to die.

These dead mesquite trees no longer retard a vigorous stand of Indiangrass.

Selling partly grown live oak and red oak trees to landscapers helps pay the cost of clearing the land.

This Caterpillar tractor and dirt wagon have been in constant use for more than sixteen years, building dams and roads on Flat Top.

April, when soil temperature was right for rapid germination. Seed was drilled into flat ground. Bedded rows were not needed because irrigation on Flat Top is done with a sprinkler system.

Seeding rate was thirty to forty pure-live-seed per row foot for sideoats grama and fifteen PLS per row foot for the tall grasses. Germination was excellent, and it is believed that two-thirds of the rate used would have given satisfactory stands.

The owner of Flat Top has a deep aversion for bare spots and has transplanted this antipathy to his men. Bare places and thin spots are seeded to adapted plants. One of the pet methods is to scatter chopped sumac or live oak sprouts over open spots to give plants a chance to recuperate. Electric fences also are used to isolate worn-out corners or other areas where plants need rest from grazing.

One of the most difficult types of ranch management practices is that of keeping the number of livestock in balance with the yearly forage production. The policy at Flat Top has been to leave almost half of the yearly grass production on the ground for conservation and improvement. Some wonder how a cow can tell when she has eaten 50 to 60 per cent. She can't, of course, but managers can, and that is where the real gift of management shows up and counts.

The weather, though varied, is favorable for successful ranching. Climate is continental in type, characterized by quick changes in temperature, marked extremes, and wide temperature ranges both daily and yearly.

January temperatures average about 46 degrees Fahrenheit; average for July is about 84 degrees; maximums are around 112 and minimums are minus 2 or 3 degrees. Average growing season is about 225 days.

Over two-thirds of the thirty-two-inch annual precipitation falls during April, May, and June. The driest period occurs in December, January, and February. Droughts of several months' duration are frequent, and some last four to five years. Snowfall is infrequent, but winter ice storms are more common. Precipitation is excellent for range and adequate for farming, but most soils on the ranch are unsuited for farming.

Since there are no high sheltering mountains, winds move freely over the prairies. Livestock find some shelter from cold winds along the hill slopes that border the stream valleys. The Norther, the Texas brand name for the brisk to fierce northerly winds that drift southward over Texas, cross over the ranch regularly, and the Blue Norther often distresses man and beast when they are caught without protection against the moisture and chilling winds that characterize this more robust type of Norther.

During the last four droughty years grass production has been only 40 to 60 per cent of what it was before. There were 2,400 registered Herefords on the ranch four years ago; in midsummer, 1956, there are about 1,000. That is why the grass is still improving; that is why the cost of feeding cows has not gone up despite the drought; that is why the ranch is making money instead of losing it by buying expensive hay and concentrates that the larger herd would have required.

A herd can always be trimmed to improve it, and Flat

Top men have used this opportunity to cut theirs down to a superior herd of breeding cows and bulls.

Grass has been a strongly influencing force in human history. The quiet strength of a healthy grassland escapes our imagination until recognition is dramatically forced upon us after some calamity or act of man deprives us of its benefits and leaves us stricken like Samson shorn of the long hair that sustained him.

On Flat Top, strength from the long grasses is renewing the soil along the creek and river bottoms where choking tree growth has been killed and land reclamation is gradually progressing. Here an astonishing thing has happened; sideoats grama, little bluestem, big bluestem, Indiangrass, and switchgrass have sprung up on tree-cleared land and are beginning to colonize. These plants, long suppressed by dense shade, survived puny and unnoticed until freed from tree competition, and then they thickened and grew up in a flush, like magic. At first they are babied and not grazed in summer until they have developed both the stand and the vigor required for safe pasturing by the Herefords.

Big bluestem, Indiangrass, and switchgrass are the favored tall grasses. They are admirably adapted to subirrigated valleys, where they occurred abundantly in the primeval grasslands of Central Texas.

These admirable grasses have a number of attributes in common: all are warm-season growers; they are tall grasses; they are sought after by cattle; they are excellent hay producers; all reproduce by seed and by rootstocks or underground stems; all have deep fibrous roots; and they are excellent soil-conservation grasses.

43

Their spectacular root systems are their key attributes for high production and survival, yet this feature is little understood by stockmen. Each of the two root types has specialized functions. The rootstock, a fleshy enlargement, produces new plants and has the additional function of storing plant food such as sugars, starches, proteins, and mineral compounds with which to nourish the grass when it starts growing following dormancy.

Many have wondered how it is possible for these grasses to survive long periods of heavy use without having an opportunity to make seed. The reason the plants live is because both rootstocks and, to a lesser extent, fibrous roots store food that maintains the life of the plants. Grasses are known to survive a long time without having a chance to develop seed provided sufficient leaves are let grow to manufacture plant food that can be stored in the roots.

These three tall grasses, also, produce masses of interlacing fibrous roots that saturate the surface one foot of soil and also send roots from five to twelve feet deep into the ground when ranges are maintained in vigorous condition. Fibrous roots also have a minor role in food storage, but function primarily as gatherers and transporters of soil moisture and minerals. Flat Top tall grasses are healthy and vigorous, hence root systems are normal and reach deeply into the soil for nutrients and water. Roots shallow up and thin out on ranges where tops are nubbed too closely by animals, hence a lot of water and minerals that are available to Flat Top grasses cannot be reached by short-rooted plants where ranges are heavily grazed.

All three grasses vary in height from two to eight feet

tall, depending upon fertility of soil and availability of water. Flowers are borne on long fruiting stalks; seedheads of big bluestem resemble a turkey's foot; seedheads of Indiangrass resemble medium-sized yellow plumes, while the seedheads of switchgrass form an open sprangle of numerous branchlets, each terminating with a brown beadlike seed. Experience has shown that these native tall grasses are the kind that a rancher can tie to. They have both the staying qualities and the producing power that the ranching business requires for success.

Approximately 90 to 95 per cent of the elements from which plants grow are obtained from the air and only 5 to 10 per cent come from the soil. A large part of that obtained from the air comes in the form of carbon and nitrogen. Plants decay and become organic matter, the substance which feeds teeming billions of living microscopic soil organisms.

The first twenty-four inches of soil supports a denser population of living matter than any other life zone in the universe. This life includes invisible plants, animals, and insects, and worms and rodents. The microscopic life converts minerals and nitrogen into available forms that the minute roots of plants absorb in a water solution. Vegetation could not survive if there were no microscopic soil life, and these organisms could not live without the organic matter that is provided by decaying plants. The land-management program at Flat Top allows these natural wonders to operate unimpeded.

Earthworms play a big role of conditioning soil and improving fertility of ranges in good and excellent condition

45

like those on Pettit's ranch. Worms live on dead vegetation, humus, and soil minerals. Part of their waste products are deposited on the soil surface as castings which have high fertilizing value.

An acre of highly productive bluestem range like that on Flat Top has as much as five to ten tons of earthworm castings deposited on the soil surface in a year, whereas the amount left on ranges in poor condition may be less than one thousand pounds per year. Organic matter content of these worm castings is 8.66 per cent compared with only 2.59 per cent in the topsoil. Nitrogen in worm castings is three times greater than in topsoil, and phosphorous in castings is four times greater; potassium is three times greater in the castings.

Not all of the native legumes have nitrifying properties, but of those that nitrify, the perennial types appear to have this propensity more than annuals. The Texas bluebonnet, a winter annual, however, is particularly good as a supplier of nitrogen. The better perennial native legumes are increasing on Flat Top ranges, those in good and excellent condition having the most.

In the process of soil leaching by water, available minerals often are deposited deeply in the subsoil. Thrifty ranges like those on the ranch have an abundance of deep-rooted grasses and forbs that tap these deeply bedded mineral supplies and deposit them in the leaves and stems of range plants. When the plants die, the unused parts finally become humus and a new source of mineral is added to the top soil. Overgrazed short-rooted grasses and forbs cannot reach either deeply bedded supplies of mineral or moisture and this loss affects the pocketbook of the ranch operator.

Some may wonder why the ranch has not resorted to wholesale fertilization of native range. The idea was considered, but Flat Top management will not buy a program that cannot pay its freight. The Soil Conservation Service tested Texas limestone ranges to find out if fertilizing paid. It was found that nitrogen increased grass yield some, phosphate increased legume yield, and both increased weed yield. However, increased range forage production failed to pay the cost of fertilizers and application. Appropriate fertilizer applications are profitable, however, on cropland.

Land enrichment is thus achieved as a bonus for good grassland management, and Flat Top's owner agrees with the unknown wise man who said, "The soil locks within its embrace the beginnings of all life and receives at last their discarded forms. It will outlive all the works of man, transcend all human thought. It traces the progress of history and shelters its ignoble end. It speaks eloquently and is dumb. It is the imperishable storehouse of eternity."

W. B. (Bill) Roberts, the ranch manager, was hired in 1941 because he was regarded as an outstanding authority on beef breeding and ranch management. If you ride with Pettit and Bill over the ranch, they will show you bunches of contented, broad-backed, deep-bodied registered Hereford cattle. With their broad, thick backs as smooth as golf greens and deep sides extending to their hocks and knees, these fine cattle resemble walking blocks of meat. Flat Top breeders have artfully bred a strain of cattle that are peers in the royal families of the Hereford kingdom. The men

47

whose skills have perfected these animals get a rich measure of their reward in the form of pride of achievement. But the deep-seated reason behind careful breeding is economy in animal production. The goal of breeding on Flat Top is greatest animal production per feed unit used or most efficient food production.

Pettit and Bill Roberts are skilled cattle judges who appreciate how changes in outside structure affect the carcass. They have selected for increased thickness of loin, rib, and quarter, for more rapid fattening tendencies, and for early maturity. By mating animals that nick well, these traits are so strongly fixed that they are transmissible. This has aided in building up the present Flat Top herd, which is famous for cattle that can live all year on native grass. They have bred also for cows that are good milkers and will turn off husky weaner calves. They have proved to their own satisfaction that inherited qualities for beef production flourish best when cattle have access to ranges in top condition. They claim that good grazing and progressive breeding programs must advance simultaneously.

Flat Top personnel have made mileage in building up excellent grazing resources and a top herd of purebred Hereford cattle. But they have accomplished something even greater by developing and building up the yielding-power of the soil, the most valuable mineral on earth. This accomplishment is of greater value than the gold that Coronado sought in the seven golden cities of Cíbola. A strong soil is basic to permanent ranching and to permanent national welfare.

Chapter 5

BRUSH AND WEED CONTROL

MARTINE EMERT

THE TEXAS SUN SHINES on millions of acres of cactus, cedar, mesquite, sumac, scrub oak, and similar woody brush, plus more millions of acres of broomweed, ragweed, and other pests where fine nourishing grasses could be growing. A few jack rabbits and rattlesnakes eke out a meager living on land that could support more cattle—if the cactus and brush were removed.

But those millions of acres of brushy and weedy low-producing ranges need not stay that way. Most of them can be reclaimed and made to support many more livestock, to produce meat for the people of the country, and to put money in the pockets of their owners. Brush covered, these acres produce far below their capability; grass covered, their value can be increased as much as ten times, and their production will pay for all the work of restoration within a few years. Then for an infinity of years to come, they will continue to bring high returns to the rancher, so long as he does not overgraze and weaken or destroy his turf.

When the white man first brought his cattle into Central Texas, he found the rolling hills covered with grasses growing three to four feet high on the rocky hilltops and much higher in the creek bottoms. There was little cactus, no cedar, no mesquite, very little sumac, scrub oak, or elm, no

49

bad weeds—only vast acreages of Indiangrass, big blue-stem, little bluestem, and sideoats grama—the finest of feed for his animals. The grass seemed limitless. As the years sped swiftly by, more and more cattle and sheep were brought in to graze the grasslands.

But little by little, changes began to take place. Too many cattle and too many sheep ate the grasses close to the ground. The vigorous roots of these grasses, burrowing deeply into the earth for minerals and moisture, were dependent upon the leaves above for plant food to sustain them. As the leaves were eaten, the roots became starved, and the plants dwindled. And because the leaves were destroyed, no seeds could be formed to grow new plants. The fine nutritious grasses began to die out, and the poorer ones came in. But the cattle and the sheep remained on the land and ate the poorer grasses too, leaving the ground poorly covered and open for the invasion of cactus, brush, and weeds. Meanwhile, much land was cleared and plowed for cotton. Year after year of cotton depleted the soil. The crop yield diminished until it was no longer worthwhile to plant. The land was abandoned—and the cactus and brush crept in on a lot of it.

But to make money in the ranching business, it is absolutely essential to have plenty of grass as the basic feed for cattle. There is little sustenance for them in the weeds and cactus, the cedar and mesquite—greedy, rapacious plants which take over the land and seize the water and nutrients needed by the grass.

Nature has a very efficient way of dealing with these bandits of the plant world, and man can do well to follow it.

Where grass grows perfectly, these invading plants are licked. The seeds of these invaders may be lying dormant, waiting for a breakdown of the turf to begin their active growth, but so long as a fine stand of healthy grass is maintained, these plants are held in check.

How can good grass stands be developed on brushy ranges? It is not easy, and it requires time and work and patience. First, the unwanted plants must be removed to give the grass the advantage of the food and moisture available in the soil. On old range land, there are frequently enough parent plants of native grasses left to produce seed to replant cleared areas if the competition is removed. However, where a range has become heavily infested with brush, the Flat Top Ranch finds it practical to overseed newly cleared land by hand with native grass seed harvested with the combine.

Second, cattle need to be kept off the grass until it has become established. This may require two or three years. Special care needs to be given young plants in a drought year when a seedling of one of the tall native grasses, such as big bluestem, can only produce a root system a few inches in depth. When cattle are allowed to graze these young plants, they pull them up, roots and all, and the ground is left bare for the weeds and brush to come in. If left undisturbed, however, the roots will penetrate a foot or more into the ground in a year or two, and are not so easily pulled up.

When it has been determined to clear a pasture of brush so that the money-making grasses can take over, the next decision is where to start. It is usually easiest to tackle the

51

shallow soils first, for these produce a less dense growth. This was done at the Flat Top Ranch, but was soon discontinued. More money can be made by clearing deep soil first and getting it into high production. There is usually more to be done, and the costs are higher than on the shallow soil, but the returns are so much greater that in the long run clearing the best land is actually the cheapest. The farmer or rancher who has only his own time and money and labor will have to work a little at a time, gradually moving from his deep soils to his shallowest, doing a complete and thorough job with each area before beginning the next. Immediately after clearing, all livestock should be kept off until the grass is firmly established. Sometimes only a portion of a pasture needs attention—perhaps a little patch of mesquite or cactus—and this small area can be temporarily protected with an electric fence. These fences are very cheap, and will turn livestock. Once the animal has felt the shock it will not approach the fence again.

The really tough weeds on Flat Top are annual broomweed and ragweeds. These weeds are shallow rooted, and can spring up easily after a half-inch rain that does not provide moisture enough to give a boost to the growth of the deep-rooted native grasses.

Weeds take a tremendous amount of moisture and food from the soil that is needed for the growth of the grass. In general, it takes about four times as much water to produce a pound of weeds as to produce a pound of grass, which means, of course, that you can get much more grass if the weeds are removed. And you can be sure the grass would thrive there, too, for you do not find weeds growing well on exhausted soils. Annual weeds depend upon water and fertility from the top few inches of soil, while grass roots grow much deeper. Since grass is excellent feed for cattle and weeds offer almost nothing in nutritional value, it doesn't take much figuring to see the terrific loss a rancher takes from the weeds growing where the grass ought to be.

But how can you get rid of the weeds? Mowing may be effective on small areas. Of course, mowing cuts back the grasses and legumes as well as the weeds, but this does little damage if done but once and will pay on those weeds which can be killed with one mowing. But most weeds will grow up again and may have to be mowed a second or even a third time in a single season. This becomes too expensive as the cost of each mowing is about $1.00 per acre. Also, successive mowings damage the good grasses and legumes. Another method is to spray weeds with a chemical known as 2,4-D, diluted with water, usually in the proportion of one hundred gallons of water to one gallon of chemical. Plants in healthy condition have considerable reserve as a necessary food supply. The hormone, 2,4-D makes a susceptible plant grow so fast it quickly uses up its reserve of sugar, and at the same time the cells enlarge so rapidly they rupture and the plant dies. This chemical in proper dosages kills broad leaved plants, including the very important legumes like hairy vetch and sweetclover, but doses strong enough to kill weeds do not harm grass. Perennial legumes and other good range forbes are set back by 2,4-D spray but are not killed by dosages adequate to kill broomweed and ragweed. If the ranges are not sprayed often, the good forbs will recover.

53

The effectiveness of this spray is dependent upon the stage of growth of the weed. The faster the plant is growing, the more easily it is killed. Spraying is particularly effective if done when the weeds are not more than a couple of inches high. A sprayer can be arranged to cover nearly one hundred acres in a day, and the cost will not exceed $1.00 per acre for labor, fuel, and chemical. If properly done, and at the right time, the kill will be 100 per cent. But the catch is that the spray will have no effect on the seeds that have not germinated, and there is always the possibility that more weeds will come up before the grass has had a chance to take over. Weeds cannot be entirely eliminated, only controlled.

In seasons of normal rainfall, especially when there is an abundance in winter and early spring, the grasses on a good pasture are usually established before the weeds get a chance to sprout. So, if all years were normal, the problem of weed control on grassy ranges would not be a very difficult one. But rainfall is not always normal. In a year such as 1955, weeds covered pastures that had not been over-grazed and had been relatively free from weeds in the past. Winter and spring were both very dry and with only an occasional light shower, which was fine for weeds but poor for grass. Then came hard freezes just at the end of March, which set back the tender grass shoots, but affected the weeds only slightly. With a head start, broomweeds and others soon overtopped the grass. Actually, grass was growing fairly well under the broomweed, but that did not minimize the problem of getting rid of the weeds—and the millions of seeds they were producing.

In the final analysis, weed control is dependent upon a thick turf of grass and moderate grazing—but overgrazing for one season can ruin the work of years. Over the long pull a good stand of climax grasses is the cheapest and most effective type of weed control.

Pricklypear is the only form of cactus which is bothersome on Central Texas ranges. Other kinds of cactus are not hard to handle, do not spread much, and do not cover much territory. Only two species of pricklypear are common in Central Texas: a small round-leaved species called Tasajillo, and the much more numerous kind with big wide blades covered with sharp spines.

Pricklypear is remarkably well specialized for invading weakened ranges. Even a small plant has a most astonishing root spread. Roots fan out in all directions only an inch or so beneath the surface. Follow one of these roots and you will see how it branches and rebranches so that the whole surface of the ground is underlain by thirsty rootlets for as much as forty feet in all directions from the parent plant. These rootlets suck in soil moisture immediately after rains. The moisture is stored in the leaves, and when the drought comes, the cactus draws on its reserve and grows while other plants weaken.

Some ranches use pricklypear to save their cattle from starvation. It is true that hungry cattle are trained to eat it; in fact, they learn to like it. In some areas ranchers have used a pear-burner, a torch that burns off the spines of the cactus so cattle can eat it better.

But here is the trouble—in spite of greatest care, some of the thorns remain and are swallowed by the cattle. They get a liking for the cactus and even eat plants from which the stickers have not been removed. These needle-pointed spines then work their way through the animal's system, piercing and penetrating vital organs.

There are two other reasons why cactus should be removed. First, it harbors rattlesnakes. Second (and this is probably the most important of all), it takes several times as much water to produce as does a pound of grass. Therefore, the rancher who keeps the cactus off his land can count on far more cattle feed from grass than he can obtain from cactus. And, most significant, the quality of grass forage is superior to that of cactus.

Since pricklypear is harmful, it should be removed and the grass given a chance to grow. Fortunately, the job is neither very difficult nor very expensive, and the government will pay a portion of the cost. Since payments vary from 60 cents to $5.00 an acre, according to the degree of infestation, those interested will want to consult the Agricultural Stabilization and Conservation Committee in their county seat to find out how much financial help can be obtained in the clearing of land.

Two cactus control methods are used at Flat Top. The first is to spray with the chemical, 2,4,5-T, mixed with Diesel oil or kerosene. The cactus must be covered with the spray to kill it. If even a little spot is left uncovered the plant will grow again. At best, you can only hope to kill about 70 per cent of the plants. Soon the other 30 per cent will grow again, and the whole control operation will have to be repeated.

At the Flat Top Ranch the use of chemical spray on

East Bosque Creek where it enters Flat Top. This picture was taken in the summer of 1956.

East Bosque Creek where it leaves Flat Top. This picture was taken in July, 1956, after six years of drought.

pricklypear has been discontinued, and plants are now grubbed out by hand. In the long run, this is much the cheaper method. It takes as much time and labor to spray as it does to grub out the plants. In addition, you will have the cost of the chemicals and not more than a 70 per cent kill can be assured. If the job of grubbing is done carefully, the kill is nearly 100 per cent.

In cactus eradication, as in every other operation of a ranch, the only inexpensive method is the one that does the job permanently. It is far cheaper to go over the ground, grubbing by hand, but doing it only once, than it is to spray quickly—and have to do it over and over again.

Labor becomes the most important element. On the Flat Top Ranch, the labor is entirely performed by local farmers during their slack work periods in winter and early spring. These men are conscientious and careful workers, and the outstanding success of the cactus eradication program is a tribute to their efforts. They work in small crews of six or seven under the direction of one of their own number. For many of these men, the extra work of Flat Top has made it possible to hold on to their small farms and feed their families through the long drought that began in 1950.

It is only practical to grub out the cactus during the winter and early spring, before the grass becomes green. At that time, it is easily seen, and none will be missed. The plant is uprooted with a grubbing hoe, and great care is taken to be sure that the "potato" is removed. This is a tuber at the base of the plant, several inches underground, that is named for its marked resemblance to an Irish potato. The roots spring out from this growth, and all the circulation of the plant goes through it, as through the human heart. All the leaves, blossoms, buds, and "potatoes" are gathered up with pitchforks and loaded onto a dump truck. Any portion of the plant left lying on the ground will take root and grow. The truck carries the cactus fragments to a clear spot, where they are dumped in a big pile. As warm weather comes on, the pile heats and the plants die. A year later, very little will be left of the heap. Occasionally a leaf will take root in the pile, but it can easily be dug out.

With the cactus gone, the grass had to be given a chance to grow. Where each cactus was removed, the men dropped a few grass seeds into the ground and stepped on them to assist the grass in getting a start ahead of the weeds. From then on, the problem of changing from a cactus to a grass cover became one of management. Cattle were kept out until a good grass cover was established. How long this required depended on many factors—the extent of the cactus infestation, the amount of grass present, the condition of the soil, the seasonal moisture. When a good turf was established, the pasture was ready for proper grazing.

So long as a heavy growth of grass is maintained on the land, cactus will not be a bother. Cactus eradication will pay for itself within one or two years in the increased yield of grass, which will mean increase of weight on good healthy cattle and higher income for better beef.

Mesquite and cactus have a lot in common. Both invade an area when the native grasses have been badly weakened or destroyed through overgrazing, and the soils have become hard and droughty through destruction of humus. Both plants take tremendous quantities of water and food

58

from the soil, thus depriving the grass of needed moisture and nourishment. An ordinary mesquite tree that is three inches in diameter will use twenty-five gallons of water each twenty-four hours if it can get it. In Central Texas, it has a root system that is about as large underground as the tree is above ground, but the more droughty the soil, the more extensive is the root system in comparison to the size of the tree. These roots not only extend out near the surface, but also burrow deeply into the ground to take up the water from that source.

The mesquite tree produces pods or beans that are nutritious livestock feed, and some people say they would rather have the beans than grass for their animals. However, to produce a gallon of beans requires one thousand gallons of water—and with this same thousand gallons of water, you can probably produce ten times as much grass as beans. This makes the beans an expensive feed for animals. But that is not all. Cattle can digest only a part of the beans, and the rest passes through them. These seeds eventually take root and produce a mesquite thicket. When the trees are at least fifty yards apart, they produce quantities of beans, but when they are only ten feet apart, they produce almost no beans at all. Mesquite is a losing proposition any way you look at it, and any rancher with these trees on his land is taking a terrific financial beating year after year that few can afford. It is a whole lot cheaper to get rid of the mesquite than to leave it there.

Some people think mesquite is hard to kill, but in reality it is very easy and relatively inexpensive, and, as with the cactus, the government will bear a part of the cost. This will vary from 14 cents to $5.00 an acre, depending upon the number of trees present.

The most difficult problem in any brush or tree eradication program is the sprouts that persist in springing up after the parent plant has been considered killed. Many people have tried bulldozing mesquite and then piling up the trees and burning them. The pastures were cleared—for a time. And then the sprouts came back thicker than before.

This is because the mesquite tree has a bud ring or bud zone below the ground line similar to the "potato" of the cactus. This is the living heart of the tree. From it the roots stretch out in all directions and the trunk or sprouts grow upward. The tree is never killed until this heart is killed. Bulldozing knocks off the top but does not always take out the heart, which may live and produce sprouts for years. The problem in killing mesquite, then, is not the problem of removing the top, but of killing the heart or bud zone.

There are a number of attachments that may be used on a bulldozer to remove the heart. One is a type of heavy knife that cuts beneath the surface and severs the roots and the bud. Another is a heavy pronged instrument which lifts the tree out of the ground, roots and all. Both methods are expensive, but fairly effective.

Pouring kerosene around the roots is another control method, but this has not been too effective on some soils, and many plants sprout again.

The most effective method at Flat Top is spraying a band around the tree trunk by hand with a hormone called 2, 4, 5-T ester, diluted with either kerosene or Diesel oil. Kerosene is less efficient as it will evaporate. The Diesel oil is heavy and sticky. It makes the chemical stay in place even during a heavy rain. This spray works on trees and shrubby growth in very much the same manner that 2,4-D does on weeds. Results have been good.

The cost of the material is surprisingly small. Various brands will require different dilutions, but the cost per acre is about the same with all of them. For instance, the spray that costs $8.75 a gallon will require dilution in the proportion of twenty to one. Diesel oil is only about 15 cents a gallon, making $3.00 for twenty gallons, or a total of $11.75 for twenty-one gallons of spray in the proper proportions. A five-gallon can, representing a little more than $2.50 in materials will cover from one-half to five acres, depending upon the density of the growth.

The job can be done by hand with a knapsack sprayer, and here again the efficiency and carefulness of the man doing the spraying is the most important factor. He uses a regular nozzle that sprays in a fan shape about two inches wide. A band six inches in width, at least a foot above the ground, should be carefully sprayed all around the trunk of the tree. At this height, any material that runs down the trunk will help kill the tree rather than be wasted by dripping on the ground. If even a tiny streak in the band is left unsprayed, the tree will continue to grow, but if the spraying is done right the kill will be nearly 100 per cent. And best of all, there are few sprouts! As with the cactus, it pays to hire careful workmen and to take the necessary time to be sure the job is done right—and do it only once. If the work is carelessly or hurriedly done, it is almost worthless and will have to be repeated in the near future. To a man with five hundred acres, such a job may seem interminable, but killing is by far the cheapest and quickest eradication program. The dead trees may be left where they are. They will disintegrate in a surprisingly short time and add their bit of organic matter to the soil to become food for the growing grass. Trees should not be burned. Not only does burning destroy the organic matter in the trees, which is needed in most pastures, but it also burns the organic matter in the topsoil, leaving it impoverished and sterile.

Like mesquite, the cedar is an invading plant that comes in when the land is overgrazed. Each tree produces thousands of berries, which cattle cannot eat but birds enjoy. The birds scatter the seeds widely, and the cedars grow wherever the grass cover is sufficiently weakened to give them a foothold. The cedar is another tree that greedily sucks up all the moisture and plant food within reach of its roots and shades out the grass. Within a surprisingly short time, a cedar thicket grows so dense that little light and little food or moisture is available for grass.

What is usually called cedar is in reality a juniper. In Central Texas, there are two common species. Originally, the red cedar (blueberry juniper) was by far the most numerous, possibly because the birds seemed to like it best. From this tree come the widely known red cedar posts used for fences over this entire section of Texas. The tree is easily destroyed. A bulldozer can be used to knock the large trees off at or below the ground, and the small trees can be dug out with a grubbing hoe. This completely kills the plant. The seeds are carried far and wide by the birds, or they may roll down the hillside thickets and infest the pastures below. It is wise to clear every cedar, even from the steepest hillslopes, in order to prevent seed from growing. Some people believe that cedars should be left growing on steep hillslopes as a protection against erosion. Actually they offer little protection, and they begin coming in only after the turf is already broken down.

The white cedar (redberry juniper) is a much more difficult pest to deal with than the red cedar. It has no value for posts, so is not subject to cutting. Its worst feature is that it has a bud ring similar to that of the mesquite, and the tree is not killed until this bud ring is removed from the ground. Therefore, it has to be dozed out by the roots or dug up with a grubbing hoe. Where the more easily controlled red cedar has been removed, the vicious white cedar has replaced it, and is probably the more prevalent now. Unless you are sufficiently familiar with the different species to tell them apart, you will probably find your best method of procedure is to bulldoze everything as deeply as possible, endeavoring to get the bud ring if it is there. If any sprouts appear, you should go over the area immediately, grubbing out the bud rings by hand before they produce another thicket. Fortunately, it is possible to get federal assistance for the cost of clearing the cedar, as with the cactus and mesquite. This assistance varies from 8 cents (for red cedar) or $1.20 (for white cedar) to $5.00 per acre.

When the cedars have been bulldozed, they should be left lying on the ground, scattered about, as they fall. This protects the bare ground from erosion until the grass can begin to grow. It is surprising that so many native grasses seem to be lying dormant under the cedars, and when given light and moisture they spring into growth. It is a good practice to bulldoze the cedars during the winter, so the grass can begin growth at the normal spring period. The development of the turf will be speeded by dropping some grass seed in each spot where a tree is uprooted and stepping on the seed so it cannot blow or wash away. The tiny grass plants will be protected by the old cedars, which in their turn disintegrate to form plant food for the grass. By the time the trees have fallen to pieces, the grass will be tall and sturdy and producing seed. The cost is negligible compared to the value of a piece of land that has been changed from a worthless cedar thicket to a fine pasture.

Eradicating cactus, cedar, and mesquite is comparatively easy, but the job on the other woody growth is frequently more complicated. However, it must be done if the rancher is to make the proper use of his land.

That means that the scrub oaks, the elms, the sumac, and all other woody underbrush should be removed to give the grass a chance to grow. Even the big trees of oak, pecan, etc., need to be reduced to a minimum, and for these special treatment is required.

Several methods have been tried for the control of these woody plants. They have been bulldozed, piled in heaps, and burned—but the sprouts have always come back. Bulldozing has been followed by goats. The goats will control the growth of the sprouts, but they overgraze the grass if too many are kept. If goats are to be used, chaining trees is preferable to bulldozing, and goating will be required for many years afterward. Bulldozing and goating have both been discontinued at the Flat Top Ranch.

A large brush cutter has been tried. This was made in Florida to cut the heavy brush in the Everglades. It resembles a cotton stalk cutter but has a big cylinder filled with water to give it weight. When filled, it weighs about 25,000 pounds and has to be pulled with a D-8 tractor. It can be used on oak and sumac, but is of little value on mesquite and cedar. At first its work seemed quite impressive—but the sprouts came back even worse than they did after bulldozing. This practice was discontinued.

Several types of small cutters that mow the brush like grass have also been tried. They break and splinter stalks up to about one and one-half inches in diameter. This has been particularly effective in killing sumac, if the sprouts are cut and splintered before the seed develops.

The cheapest and most effective method of tree-killing is hand-cutting followed by spraying. On the Flat Top Ranch, the same little crews of local farmers who grub cactus in the winter and early spring cut brush in their slack periods during the rest of the year. All brush under four inches in diameter is cut off and the stumps sprayed with 2,4,5-T. Tree trunks are girdled, and the cut space sprayed with 2,4,5-T, which will kill the tree. Ten per cent may resprout and require a second spraying.

The importance of grass to control all undesirable plants can never be overrated. Good grass will help control growth of weeds, cactus, cedar, mesquite, and other woody plants. Without the grass, the fight is unending; with the grass, the fight is simpler. So long as the proper turf is maintained, the other plants have greater difficulty in getting a foothold.

Chapter 6

FLAT TOP WATER AT WORK

J. C. DYKES

~~~~

FLAT TOP WATER is always hard at work—producing grass for the Herefords, fish for the ranch family table and for sport, a garden for the ranch family, grass seed for planting on the ranch and for sale, hay for winter feed, and sudan and Johnsongrass for summer grazing to permit the permanent pastures to rest. The direct demands for water are also heavy on the ranch. In July, 1956, there were 1,000 Herefords to be watered (there were nearer 2,500 before the dry years started in 1951). Deer, antelope, and wild turkeys plus much smaller game make it their year-round home, and an abundant supply of clean water is one of the major reasons for their permanent residency. The hog and quail projects and the cow horses all make their daily demands on the ranch water supply. The domestic demands are considerable since a sizable ranch family is necessary to its operation. Yes, the water at Flat Top is at work, but then so is everything else and everybody, which is as it should be on a practical cow ranch.

The time to appraise the efficiency of a ranch water system is during the dry years. July, 1956, was a particularly appropriate time. Flat Top was in its sixth year of below normal rainfall. It is in the same general rainfall belt as Fort Worth, and while the Weather Bureau records at Fort

66

Worth usually top those of the six rain gauges at the ranch, there are years when the ranch has slightly more rain. The normal rainfall at Fort Worth is 33.69 inches per year—the high month is usually May with a norm of 4.92 inches, and the low is August with 1.88 inches. The Fort Worth norm can be assumed to be about right for the ranch. Because of the usual rainfall pattern in Texas—progressively heavier from west to east—a more realistic norm for Flat Top would seem to be 32 inches a year.

There was only a trace of moisture recorded at Fort Worth in December, 1950, and in 1951 the drought hit the ranch in earnest. The rainfall at Fort Worth and at the headquarters gauge at Flat Top for the period January 1, 1951, to June 30, 1956, as shown in the following table, indicates the seriousness of the drought the ranch has experienced.

Year	Fort Worth	Flat Top	Shortage at Flat Top based on estimated norm of 33.69 at Fort Worth and 32 at Flat Top
1951	23.37	14.98	17.02 to 18.71 inches
1952	22.69	18.13	13.87 to 15.56 inches
1953	24.74	19.11	12.89 to 14.58 inches
1954	19.55	13.71	18.29 to 19.98 inches
1955	25.16	27.00	5.00 to 6.69 inches
First half 1956	11.82	12.00	4.00 to 4.85 inches
Total	127.33	104.93	71.07 to 80.37 inches

A shortage of seventy to eighty inches, more than the

total expected in two years, in a five and one-half year period is bound to decrease the total water supply of the ranch. The situation in mid-July 1956, was this: the beautiful green range of the uplands in May was, for the most part, brown, and a good growth of grass was curing, but the bottomland fields were still producing vigorous growths of alfalfa, sudan, and Johnsongrass, as well as Indiangrass, big bluestem, and other native grasses. There was no shortage of water for humans, livestock, or wildlife. The several springs examined were all flowing, and there was water behind all the major dams except two—one newly constructed, and Perch Lake, which will be discussed later in this chapter. The reservoirs were not full, of course, but there was water to irrigate the ranch garden and to irrigate or sub-irrigate the nearly one thousand acres of bottom land. This was all Flat Top water, for South Bosque Creek, the main natural drainageway of the ranch, was bone dry on July 12 where it entered the ranch from the north. The bed of the river was powdery and did not look as if it had been even moist for days.

The favorable water situation at the ranch is simply another example of the careful planning of the owner. He knew that a continuous supply of good water in adequate amounts, even during the driest years, was a must in building a permanent ranch. The system installed (and it is still being improved) has stood the test of time and of drought. The major water developments on the ranch are twenty-four wells and forty-three impounding dams of all sizes.

The ranch is divided into about one hundred enclosures,

ranging from small traps to one pasture containing about one thousand acres. Nearly all the pastures and fields are grazed sometime during the year, and this means water must be available in each for the livestock. For the most part, the wells are located on high points on the ranch. On the more level upland areas, water can usually be found at thirty feet in the underlying Paluxy Sand. However, the hill locations of the wells, plus the desire to tap a deeper underground reservoir with a more abundant and constant supply of water, has resulted in the wells being drilled at least two hundred feet.

Mr. Pettit believes that it is cheaper to spend a few more dollars for the deeper wells so the water can flow by gravity to the nearby pastures than to have shallower wells in the lowlands and pump the water to the higher grazing areas. He is dead set against one of his animals walking off any weight to get to water, and the water developments on the ranch make it unnecessary. But let him tell it in his own words: "It is seldom that an animal is over one-half mile from water on Flat Top—and never is the distance to good clean water over three-quarters of a mile."

There are windmills over eighteen of the wells, and there are electric pumps on the other six. It is seldom that the wind does not blow part of the day on the prairie, and there is a substantial rock and cement or concrete storage tank, that will hold a ten-day water supply, near each well for emergency use and to feed the water, through pipes, by gravity, to the concrete water troughs in the various pastures served by that particular well. And if a stillness settles over the Flat Top part of the Lampasas Cut Plain, there are the wells where the water is pumped by electricity and the *running water* in the East Bosque and its tributaries, Rough Creek, and Flag Branch, and in Tough Creek—a direct tributary of the main Bosque. The fourteen residences, the four stock barns, and the eight breeding and calving barns are all supplied with water by gravity from the twenty-four wells. Well houses, storage tanks, and water troughs are all of the same sturdy, permanent-type construction that characterize the rest of the ranch improvements. They were put there to stay.

It is well known that livestock like living or running water, and during the months the animals are in the bottom land fields, and in some of the other pastures and traps year-round, they have access to it. There are five stream miles of the East Bosque on Flat Top, and while no water was coming onto the ranch from the creek as it entered from the north, it became a living stream not long after crossing the boundary. And it was flowing a half-mile below the south boundary of the ranch on July 14, 1956—after five and one-half years of short rainfall!

One of the major arguments that has raged through the irrigated west over the years is on water yields. In many places, the irrigation farmers have opposed the application of conservation practices on the range along the upper reaches of the streams supplying them with water. They feared that water conservation measures on the upland ranges would mean a greater growth of grass and thereby a greater consumptive use of water. This, they argued, would result in less water for irrigation downstream. For example, it was not until 1954 that the State Soil Conservation District Enabling Act of the state of Arizona was amended to permit the inclusion of range lands within district boundaries. Meanwhile, the irrigation farmers of Arizona had enjoyed the benefits of organized conservation effort in districts for fifteen years. Arizona ranchers and irrigation farmers have settled their differences, but the argument goes on elsewhere. In nearly any small watershed project proposed in the West involving irrigation water supply, the controversy is almost sure to break out anew.

In July, 1956, one of Mr. Pettit's neighbors, living below Flat Top on the East Bosque, came to him to say, "I was pretty sore when you started building dams on the East Bosque, but, by God, you've made it into a flowing stream the year round. It always went dry during the summer when we had droughts before." While there was no reason to doubt this good neighbor, this was something that had to be seen. On July 14, 1956, Mr. Pettit and this writer, drove to the lower of the five dams on the East Bosque. We left the car, left the ranch by climbing through the fence, and some hundred yards or so below the dam, found a place where we could descend the rather steep bank to the bed of the stream. There was flowing water where we reached the stream bed, and as we followed it downstream the flow seemed to increase. Finally it was too wet for us to walk and we turned back.

The changing of the East Bosque from a dry to a flowing stream as it crosses the ranch from the northwest to the southeast is not a miracle or even a mystery. Flat Top *grass* and Flat Top *dams* are responsible. They are also responsible for making Rough Creek and Flag Branch year-long flowing streams. 71

Flat Top grass is the most important factor in the changed water situation. Charles Pettit says, "Water is the thing that the ranching country runs short of too often. But there is one sure way to make the best use of the rain we get and that is get the ground coated with a heavy grass sod so that the water can quickly soak into the soil."

No truer words were ever spoken because there is good evidence, developed by the Soil Conservation Service on bluestem ranges near the ranch, to prove Pettit's claims. It was found that two or three thousand pounds of well-distributed air-dry grass per acre will let most of the rain that falls sink quickly into the soil. Some water from exceptionally heavy rains will run off, but heavy losses will seldom occur from good grass sod.

Either dead or living vegetation serves satisfactorily for cover. Dead stems and leaves, the course butts of grass too tough for forage, make excellent soil cover.

Most Flat Top pastures have more than the minimum amount of plant cover required for soil protection. Under the sound grazing system being practiced, the thick absorbent litter checks the dashing rain and converts it into harmless spray that soon soaks into the soil. The good grass cover has been so effective in controlling runoff that several of the earliest constructed small stock ponds have dried up.

Together, runoff and evaporation used to get most of the water that fell on the ranch, but now rains soak into the ground to grow grass, and a considerable amount seeps slowly into underground channels, and part of it eventually reaches the natural drains (the stream beds) or breaks out as springs. Protective plant cover reduces evaporation losses

A ramp with a track and winch enables one man to lower the motor and pumping unit down to the water's edge at all times, or raise it in case of high water.

Windmill and water storage tank near barn and working corral.

Switchgrass and Johnsongrass are subirrigated by one of the many lakes built at Flat Top.

The irrigated fields produce abundant crops of alfalfa, grain, and grass.

to a minimum; growing vegetation gets the use of a large part of the total rain because it soaks deeply into the soil reservoir, where it is recovered by plants as needed.

Weedy trees, weedy grasses, and forbs are water-hogs and water-wasters, and the ranch has reduced these to a minimum. Good grass has crowded out wasteful weeds, and tree and brush clearing programs have rid the ranch of most of its water-wasting woody plants. The non-commercial types that have been cleared away are wanton users of water, requiring about twice the amount to produce a pound of dry matter as good grass. The grass makes money, the useless woody plants only make trouble. Also, the very deep-rooted woody plants draw water from deep underground sources, which eventually feed springs and creeks. It has been estimated that in Texas more water is transpired annually into the sky through the leaves of worthless woody vegetation than runs off all Texas rivers into the Gulf of Mexico. Large scattered live oak trees have been left for cattle shade, and around 5,000 pecans have been left along the creek bottoms.

The effectiveness of grass in causing in-soak of rainfall was also clearly demonstrated on the ranch some years back. A dam was constructed on an unnamed, usually dry, draw. Using the title, "Ruining a Fishing Hole," Frank Reeves wrote a delightful little essay about what happened. It is well worth preserving and here it is as he wrote it:

Perch Lake at Flat Top Ranch once was a dependable year-round watering place for cattle even during dry years. That is not the case any more.

J. C. Dykes

It is not unusual for something to happen to a tank or lake to destroy its usefulness for watering cattle. The dam may bust or the water basin may fill from erosion of the soil in its drainage area to mention only a few of the hazards. None of these happened to Perch Lake to end its usefulness as a source of supply for stock water. Instead the grass became too dense and tall in its drainage area.

When the lake was built the supply of grass at Flat Top Ranch was meager to fair. During years of normal rainfall the lake would fill two or three times a year and run around the spillway. When Pettit purchased the ranch he had a head full of ideas that were focused to improving the quantity and quality of the ranch grasses.

The late R. J. Kinzer (American Hereford Association, Kansas City, Mo.) was a very close personal friend of Pettit. He frequently advised with Pettit about his Hereford breeding program. He was always busy, but when he had the time he would visit with Pettit and rest.

Both Pettit and Kinzer liked to fish. Pettit gave the lake its name and stocked it with fish. It was a treat to watch and listen to these two friends as they used their fly rods in Perch Lake. There was always a lot of good natured banter back and forth between them, but they caught plenty of fish.

Pettit had started his range improvement program. He figured the water that fell on the sloping drainage area for Perch Lake ran off before it had time to sink into the ground and provide moisture to grow the grass. He reasoned he could correct this by a series of furrows to retard the flow of the water. The furrows were about four feet apart. They were not deep or wide and did very little damage to the existing grass turf. They were run on the contour of the drainage area.

This program retarded the water much better than Pettit had anticipated. The grass began to spread and grow in height. Soon there was a dense growth of grass and it helped to hold back the water and give it time to go into the ground. That was the beginning of the end. It spelled doom for Perch Lake as a hot fishing hole and a dependable stock water supply.

The first year Perch Lake failed to fill it was charged to spotty rain conditions that missed that area. The next year the water in the lake became progressively less and the grass in the drainage area much better. A check of the ranch rain gauges helped to determine the cause for Perch Lake going dry.

Yes, Pettit lost a good fishing spot but he did not regret it. He had found a way for growing more grass for his Herefords. He could build other fishing holes easier than he could buy feed for the cattle.

While all the dams that impound water are an important part of the ranch improvement program, those constructed on the East Bosque (five) and on its tributaries, Rough Creek (six) and Flag Branch (six), are making the greatest contributions. Water backs up in the stream channels along the gentle valleys from one dam to the downstream toe of the dam above it in the series. This has restored the water table in the valleys where formerly flash runoff from the denuded uplands had cut deep trenches in which the streams flowed. After the flood runoff passed, the deeply entrenched channels served as drains which lowered the water table. Approximately two hundred acres of land will eventually be subirrigated by the restored water table in these valleys. Well over one hundred acres have already been reclaimed. As these fertile valleys have been cleared of scrub trees and brush, the tall native grasses have taken over. Now these valley meadows, if not cut, could hide a cow herd in summer. But the Flat Top management had other plans for these subirrigated native grass meadows. They were cut for hay in May (1956) and were not used

75

again until they set a seed crop. The seed was harvested in October or November. The cattle were turned in early in November and grazed until about April 1. A hay crop, grass seed (selling for about $1.00 a pound in 1956), and four to five months grazing each twelve months will quickly amortize the cost of the dams.

One other dam is worthy of special mention—it impounds House Lake. It is on an unnamed draw just below Rock House. House Lake provides the water for the irrigation of the ranch garden plus a small trap located below the dam. Guests at Flat Top will all testify to the excellence of vegetables made possible by Flat Top water—and to the quality of fish caught in Flat Top water and of Flat Top beef and—but, why go on? In July, 1956, the seven Herefords grazing the trap below the dam weren't keeping up with the irrigated grass.

Charlie Pettit has a real affection for his impounded water. He puts it this way, "An acre of water is worth much more to me than an acre of land." This is his way of saying that an acre of land will produce only its quota of grass, hay, or feed, while a surface acre of water (usually several acre-feet) can be used to irrigate or subirrigate several acres, with much greater production the result.

The reservoirs back of the dams will impound well over three thousand acre-feet of water in normal years. This will permit the irrigation of about eight hundred acres of bottom and benchland along the streams in addition to the two hundred acres which will be subirrigated. The feed, hay, and grazing produced by this thousand acres, with the help of added water as needed, may approach the total of the forage produced on the rest of the ranch. The owner states, "I consider the thousand acres of irrigated and sub-irrigated land to be equal in value to the sixteen thousand acres of grazing land on the ranch."

Sprinkler irrigation, with the water distributed through portable pipes, is used on the bottom land fields, meadows, and pastures, which are not sub-irrigated. Approximately five thousand feet of eight-inch steel pipe is buried in the ground and has outlets at the proper intervals for hooking up the portable pipe. The portable pipe is of aluminum, light but strong, and one section is easily handled by one man. There are about ten thousand feet of four-, five-, and six-inch sizes available on the ranch, along with three pumps to lift the water from the reservoirs. Nine acres a day can be irrigated with the excellent equipment available. The amount of water applied varies with the plants to be irrigated. For example, the sixty-eight-acre alfalfa field usually receives about three inches of water per irrigation, four times a summer, whereas a native grass meadow to be left to go to seed after the first cutting may be irrigated only once or twice, depending on the summer rainfall pattern. Whatever the water needs, Flat Top has been able to meet them, even in 1956, the sixth year the rainfall has been short.

The irrigation system is constantly being improved. One of the most recent improvements is an irrigation canal, thirty to forty feet wide and approximately a mile long, constructed along the valley of the East Bosque, about three hundred yards from the stream on the average. The ditch will be supplied with water from Big Lake (impounded by the uppermost dam in the chain on the East Bosque)

through a pipe line. Water will flow through this canal year
long and will irrigate the Blackwell switchgrass and Indiangrass planted along its banks and will assist in subirrigating
the land between the ditch and the river. Water flowing
out the lower end of the canal will find its way back into
the creek.

Another irrigation improvement was installed in July,
1956, that involved raising or lowering the height of the
pump in accordance with the level of the water in the reservoir. The pump moves on a track laid on steel pipes set on
a slab of concrete that slants from the ground level of the
field to be irrigated down to the estimated lowest level of
the reservoir at which water will be pumped. A hand winch
with a steel cable attached to the pumping unit makes it
possible for one man to raise or lower the pump. This is a
unique idea, so far as this writer knows, worked out at Flat
Top to save labor, to protect the pump, and to increase
pumping efficiency.

The ranch dams are like every other improvement on
the ranch—they look as if they are there to stay. Nearly all
of them were completely built with ranch labor, power, and
equipment. In a few cases, a little outside help was hired.
The spillways are adequate and the earthwork well done.
There is a draw-down tube through each dam on the major
drains, which permits the release of water from the upper
reservoirs in the chain to the stream channels and on into
the lower reservoirs when water is needed for the livestock,
for irrigation, or for maintaining the water level in the subirrigated meadows.

Flat Top is not the only beneficiary of the water conservation and management program which has been installed on it. The establishment of a year-long flow in dry years on the East Bosque has already been discussed. What has happened on it will not settle the arguments between the various water users in other parts of the West, but it is mighty conclusive for the Lampasas Cut Plain, where the rainfall, geology, and soil are those of Flat Top. The lowest dam in the series on the East Bosque is only a few yards from the south boundary fence, and Mr. Pettit owns the land on only one side of the river. The dam was built entirely at his expense, but he has reached an agreement with his neighbors on the other side of the river that will permit them to irrigate from the reservoir it created on the making of small annual payments. When the ranch has recovered one-half the cost of the dam, it will become the joint property of those who participate in the plan. One neighbor has definitely decided to take advantage of this opportunity to irrigate.

Perhaps the greatest unearned increment will accrue to those farmers and ranchers who live downstream on the East Bosque. For some distance they are going to have almost complete protection from floodwater damage to their bottom land fields and improvements. Until tributaries of sufficient size and number to put water over the banks enter the creek below the Flat Top boundary, there will be no floods.

Right now, as strong national interest is being directed toward watershed development and flood prevention, this achievement in converting the East Bosque into a perennial stream is a work of mighty significance. Flat Top ranch does not loom large on a Texas map; it is several times smaller on a United States map. But think what it would mean to this water-short country if the millions of watersheds that make up the nation had conservation treatment applied like that given to the East Bosque, a small tributary of the Brazos River, which drains into the Gulf of Mexico. Think what it would mean to Dallas and Fort Worth, where water supplies are shaky, to have all the formerly perennial tributaries of the upper Trinity River pouring fresh clear water all year into the city reservoirs.

Landowners have the major responsibility for watershed management. But stability of the watershed is of great significance to cities, business, industry, transportation, and recreational interests—in fact, to all of us.

A watershed is more than an area of land drained by a stream and its tributaries. It is a functional resource unit of soil, water, plant and animal life, and of the people who live on the watershed and use its resources for their various needs. Everyone lives on a watershed; every town and city is on one.

The nation has started a gigantic program of water resource development and water husbandry. In sizing up this national program in terms of the kind of a job that has already been done on Flat Top and needs to be done elsewhere, Donald A. Williams, Administrator of the United States Soil Conservation Service in Washington, has the following to say:

The critical water situation we unquestionably have been facing further points up the fact that efficient water utilization is

80

the key to resource conservation. It calls for teamwork in doing everything we can throughout the length and breadth of the watershed to conserve and develop water supplies and allied resources. It requires a practical combination of well-planned measures to cope with the many interrelated problems of over-developed groundwater, wasteful surface water runoff, flooding and sedimentation, the dissipation of precious water by useless vegetation, and other water 'leaks.'

Protecting the watershed is fully compatible with down-stream, or valley, water use. There is no reason to neglect con-servation measures that slow down wasteful and damaging watershed runoff.

It isn't the total amount of water that counts, but the *usable* amount that gets to where it is needed and is put to full use. Thus flash flood waters off of denuded ranges carry sediment into storage reservoirs and distribution systems, and thereby reduce at least the potential amount of usable water. The usable water supply can be enhanced and stabilized, on the other hand, as has been proved by repeated experience, by reducing the rate of watershed runoff.

This is not a matter of 'locking up' the water that falls on or flows over the watershed. It is, rather, a question of employing practices that encourage the water to flow down to the points of ultimate use without doing needless flood and other damage in the process, while at the same time serving the equally im-portant function of providing moisture for forage production and livestock water. I doubt if there is anyone who would seri-ously consider it anything but short-sighted to allow your water-sheds to deteriorate into eroded roof-tops, so to speak, just to speed the flow of water down across them into the valleys.

The ever enlarging need for water will eventually cost the nation billions to provide, but water is essential, and the benefits will repay costs, as has already been proved at Flat Top.

81

J. C. DYKES

About 83 per cent of our available water comes from surface sources and 17 per cent comes from ground water. The fact that surface water provides the bulk of supplies used makes land treatment practices, supplemented by flood control structures on small tributaries, even more important in watershed conservation programs.

Successful results from numerous creek watershed programs have shown that national water development should originate from an upstream conservation base rather than apply only to big stream reclamation. This involves treating land and water as a unit rather than merely conveying rain from where it falls to a reservoir. This has been done on the ranch. The water is being astutely conserved, managed, and used.

An enlarged picture of a Flat Top pasture, showing some fine whitefaces in knee-high grass near a stock pond, hangs on the wall of the conference room of the Soil Conservation Service in the South Agriculture Building in Washington, D. C. For some half-dozen years now, this writer has been careful each Friday morning at eleven o'clock when in Washington to find a place at the conference table facing the Flat Top picture. The Administrator's staff conference lasts only an hour, but despite the usually interesting discussions, there is always time for a look at the Flat Top scene. If there is a twinge of nostalgia for the Texas homeland in the weekly look, there is also a reminder that there in the picture is the rancher's trinity—good *grass*, well-bred *cattle*, and an abundance of clean *water*. No ranch can be prosperous without the three—the foundation of a permanent ranch.

Chapter 7

FLAT TOP FARMING

MARTINE EMERT

G. O. HEDRICK

A RANCH HAND is no longer just "a hired man on horseback" at Flat Top or any other well-managed ranch. The common-sense decision that large winter weight losses by cattle are wasteful and unnecessary leads to the decision that it is profitable, when soil and climate permit, to produce as much of the needed supplemental winter feed as possible on the ranch. Therefore, some of the ranch workers are engaged in farming activities, at least part time. Sudan, alfalfa, oats, Madrid sweetclover, and button clover are the only cultivated crops raised on Flat Top, and these are solely for feed for the livestock and for soil improvement. Although crops occupy but 5 per cent of the ranch lands, they are very important in the ranch economy. Grass is the basic feed for the cattle the year round, but in the climate of the Lampasas Cut Plain, there are periods when most of the native grasses are dry and low in feeding value, particularly protein. Supplemental feeds are used when the native grasses are dormant, and perhaps as important, the crop lands are grazed for short periods, and the feeds they produce are used to permit the deferment and improvement of native grass.

The acres to be farmed have been selected with care.

83

Each tract must meet one basic requirement: It must be capable of being tilled year after year, under proper conservation practices, without its productive capacity being diminished.

As each new tract was added to the Flat Top acreage, its potentialities were carefully studied. Out of the 3,400 acres originally cropped, only 800 are now in cultivation, but with good farming practices, they are yielding more than the entire 3,400 formerly produced.

To ascertain soil type, depth, and slope, a survey was made by the Soil Conservation Service. No soil was retained for farming unless it was at least eighteen inches deep and could be chiseled with a deep subsoil tiller. No land was chiseled where there was danger of cutting through into sand or gravel, which would make the area incapable of holding water.

Level land is best for most types of farming, but there is very little on the ranch. Some on which the rise is not more than one foot within one hundred feet of distance (1 per cent slope) is available, but most is between 1 and 2 per cent slope. Practically none over 2 per cent is cultivated. In addition to selection of land on the basis of soil depth and slope, the farmed areas are all easily accessible and well drained.

A great deal of attention has been given to the possibilities of irrigation. At present around four hundred acres are irrigated, using two methods—the ordinary overhead sprinkler system and subirrigation—but when the planned water system is completed, nearly one thousand acres can be economically watered.

Flat Top Farming

Subirrigation can be used in a limited number of places and, where feasible, is much less expensive than sprinklers. The many dams which have raised the level of the surface water in the lakes and streams have also raised the level of the water table. On the gently sloping land adjacent to the water, the subsoil is permanently moist within reach of plant roots and is used as any other irrigated field, yielding excellent crops at no further expense.

Flag Branch, a creek so small one can step across it, has ten dams, backing up water for subirrigation of forty or fifty acres. All of the subirrigated acres on the ranch are now growing native grasses, much of which will be used for seed production. During extremely dry weather, when the upland pastures furnish only minimum growth, these spots are lush with stands two to four feet tall.

Overhead irrigation is now used on 250 acres. The impounded water is lifted directly upon the land by pumps placed as near the lake level as possible. Three large fields have underground mains, and all use portable aluminum pipe with sprinkler heads. All irrigation equipment has paid for itself many times over in increased crop yields.

In rebuilding fertility, Flat Top followed certain basic fundamental principles. The very first was to run soil tests on the areas to be worked. Most of the cultivated land was deficient in phosphorus and nitrogen, and under some conditions, the potassium was not readily available.

Commercial fertilizers are used to grow such soil-building crops as deep-rooted legumes. Their powerful roots penetrate the hard-packed earth, breaking it up and opening numerous passages for the entrance of water and air

85

which the plant must have to survive and grow. Most important, the legumes take nitrogen from the air and turn it into nitrates in the form needed by growing vegetation, something no other plant can do. This change is effected by minute bacteria found in tiny knobs or nodules which grow only on the roots of the legumes. To make sure the necessary bacteria are present, all seeds are inoculated just before planting. When the legumes die or (preferably) are plowed under, the nitrogen remains in the soil to be used by succeeding crops, such as sudan or small grain.

Legume planting has been very successful. After a thorough preparation of the ground, superphosphate, at the rate of one hundred pounds of 50 per cent super per acre, is placed in a combination drill with the legume seed. By pulling a packer behind the drill, fertilizing, planting, and packing are completed in one operation, making the job quite inexpensive.

Different legumes were used for different stages of the soil-building program, the first being Austrian winter peas planted in the fall. They were not pastured the first winter, for the weight of the heavy animals tends to pack the ground. All of the pea growth was put back into the ground for conversion into nitrogen and organic matter.

Afterward, hairy vetch (another fall-planted legume) was used with rye, oats, or barley as a nurse crop. This was pastured from the first of December until the middle of February, when the animals were taken off, so the plants could make as much growth as possible before being plowed under the first of May. A lot of soil was improved with vetch, and this practice changed many Flat Top acres from non-profitable to profitable production. One area, in particular, was near the show barn, where the soil was as hard as concrete. Nothing seemed to do any good until vetch was tried. Now the land is soft and mellow and growing good crops.

As the fertility improved, the soil-building crop was changed from vetch to sweetclover, particularly Madrid, a biennial yellow-flowered variety, which grows well under drought conditions, produces a seed crop for cash income, can be pastured or baled for hay, and when plowed under, adds nitrogen and organic matter to the soil.

Most of the irrigated land not in grass is planted to alfalfa for grazing and hay. This is one of the most important crops grown on the ranch, for it is highly palatable and nutritious, rich in protein, minerals, and vitamins, besides being a legume and a soil-builder of extraordinary merit.

Prior to the first planting, the land was chiseled to hasten the penetration of water, and then fertilized with eighty pounds of available superphosphate to the acre. Once the roots are down they probably do more than the subsoiler to open up and aerate the soil.

During the very dry year of 1955, three alfalfa cuttings yielded from three and one-half to a maximum of six tons per acre, plus grazing which was equal to more than a ton of hay. This came from a first-year planting, and one cutting was lost due to a late spring freeze. With deeper roots and no freezing, future crops may yield as much as six to eight tons to the acre in four cuttings.

Alfalfa is an important forage for all classes of cattle. Cattle graze it lightly during the winter and are taken off

87

about the middle of March. The land is renovated in late winter, and the plants spring up again to produce another four cuttings the next summer.

Corn has never been a major crop, because it usually can be purchased from Illinois or Iowa and trucked to the ranch cheaper than it can be grown. The span of time between the last frost and first hot weather is frequently too short for corn to make. Raising corn for silage is another matter, however, as it can be cut and put in silos before the hot winds burn up the crop. The first efforts at growing silage on dry land yielded only two to four tons to the acre, but corn, following two years of alfalfa, produced twelve tons to the acre on irrigated land. Some shelled corn is placed in the creep feeders for the calves in the winter time, but it is used primarily for priming out bulls and show cattle.

Button clover, a winter annual legume that is rapidly gaining favor, is another plant grown on irrigated acres. Being a medic, it resembles alfalfa in appearance and feeding value. It is self-seeding on cropland and grows well with small grain. The seed pods look like buttons, are flat, and lie close to the ground. Buttons contain about ten seeds, which are carried by the wind, water, or animals so they spread rapidly over a pasture. Seeds ripen in July, and on one field where the clover had been plowed under and came up volunteer, about $300 worth of seed was harvested per acre in 1955.

About four hundred acres are devoted to dry land farming. Because all of the fields selected for cultivation were low in fertility at the time of purchase, the same soil-building practices were necessary as were used on the irrigated

Indiangrass in blossom. This grass grows as high as eight feet along the subirrigated valleys on Flat Top.

The first cutting of this subirrigated bluestem meadow produced three tons of excellent hay to the acre.

fields. Oats, sudan, and Madrid sweetclover are the only crops grown on these non-irrigated fields, and a complete rotation program has been worked out and maintained in order to increase soil fertility.

Because the farmland is so nearly level, and because it is planted to intertilled crops only, field terraces are not necessary. On long slopes, or where breaks occur, diversion terraces are used, and many of the roads are also constructed to serve as diversion terraces. Every drop of rain that falls is needed in order to make farming possible, but thunderstorms creating five-inch rains also occur which produce runoff that must be controlled and saved for reuse.

Diversion terraces were an important first step in the reclaiming of much land. Their purpose is to control flood waters in areas where the natural drainages cross fields. The terrace consists of a low ridge built at right angles to the slope, with a broad, flat channel having a grade so slight the water will either soak in or move slowly enough that it will not cut gullies. If possible, the water that does run off is diverted to a permanent pasture where it helps to produce more grass.

Sudan is a hardy summer annual, is cheap to raise, makes rapid growth with little moisture, is highly palatable and nutritious, and produces greater yields than native grasses. Usually about thirty acres are planted to sudan. Since seed costs around $3.00 an acre and thirty acres will take care of about seventy-five head of cattle, it furnishes economical pasture. The animals are so fond of it that care must be taken not to overgraze. Cattle should not be allowed to graze it closer than six inches during the growing season.

Excepting under very adverse conditions, sudan makes some growth during the hot, dry summer months, when it is most necessary that the native grasses be deferred to permit them to make seed and develop strong root systems.

The amount of sudan pasture produced in one summer is remarkable, and hay is frequently cut. One sixty-five-acre field of sudan was grazed by eighty-four head of cattle from the time it was six inches high until it was killed by frost. During that time, it actually grew faster than the cattle could eat it. In order to set it back, a little over two tons of hay per acre were baled from two cuttings.

Seed production has been another source of income from sudan. In 1955, twenty-five acres, on which no grazing had been permitted, yielded 60,000 pounds of seed. Since this sells for 10 cents a pound, the gross income was $6,000 or $240 per acre.

Oats, planted for winter grazing, has become another important crop. Rotating oats and sudan with a soil-building legume is a good practice. There are several methods of planting and several possible rotations, but a favorite is to drill Madrid sweetclover, with the necessary superphosphate, into oats in the fall, thus cutting the machinery costs by fertilizing and seeding two crops all in one operation. This is followed after the second year by sudan.

The oats provide supplementary winter grazing in the same manner that sudan provides extra forage in the summer. With oat grazing, low-grade roughage may be used instead of alfalfa hay, thus cutting feeding costs with no loss of weight or health to cattle. If the cattle are taken off the first of March, an oat crop can be harvested, under normal weather conditions.

After the oats are off, the Madrid sweetclover, a biennial, takes over and can be used for grazing. Sweetclover is especially valuable because it will grow well under the droughty conditions often common in July and August. For the second year of the rotation, there are two choices. If seed is not to be harvested, sweetclover may be grazed the entire season, but if seed is wanted, no grazing can be permitted the second summer. Under normal conditions, the yield will be about two hundred to five hundred pounds an acre, selling for about 50 cents a pound. The seed is harvested in midsummer, and the cattle turned in to graze on the stubble, in which is usually found both Johnsongrass and annual grasses. Late in the winter, the soil is prepared for the planting of sudan the next spring. This type of rotation is used on most of the irrigated fields and maintains the soil fertility and productivity at a high level, without sacrificing its condition.

In good years, the oats are thrashed and fed to calves in creep feeders, and form the basic ingredient in the feeding ration. When the weather is too dry and the oats do not fill, the crop is cut and baled for hay.

The farming program at Flat Top is doing what it should do on a soundly operated ranch where cattle is the major enterprize—it is providing a dependable supply of forage to supplement range grazing and sale bull conditioning.

Chapter 8

THE RECLAMATION OF THE CURETON PLACE

MARTINE EMERT

G. O. HEDRICK

"IT's ABOUT THE sorriest piece of land I have ever seen," was the unhappy observation of Charles Pettit, as he surveyed the old Cureton place, the most recent addition to Flat Top, added to the southeastern portion of the ranch in 1948.

The 587 acres of once virgin prairie looked ragged and beaten. The old cropland was high in weeds and brush. On the range land, the hungry animals had eaten the sparse grass down to a few scattered nubs, and sumac, elm, scrub oak, and cactus infested the scarred slopes of the gently rolling hills. The bottom land was overgrown with trees and brush and vines, and a poor little corn field was so depleted that it yielded only a pitiful return for the labor expended upon it.

The cropland needed to be taken out of cultivation and reseeded to native grasses. But the range land—perhaps the best plan would be to fence it to keep all animals off, and just forget it as far as grazing was concerned for at least three years.

This was done. When the range land was rested, some tall prairie grasses—big bluestem, little bluestem, Indiangrass, and sideoats grama—made a surprise appearance the first growing season. On the medium and deep soils, the recovery was much more rapid than on the more shallow and eroded tracts of land.

The story of the Cureton place is the story of a thousand farms and ranches in Texas—except that this one has a happy ending. But all the stories could have happy endings if only the men who work the land would transform the worn-out fields and brush-covered pastures back into money-making crop and grass lands. On most of the land, it can be done. The cost is small compared to the value gained.

To a young soldier returning from the Mexican War to his home in Franklin County, Arkansas, the vast prairies of Central Texas, with their wooded creek bottoms, spelled opportunity and prosperity.

James Jackson Cureton, better known as Captain Jack, withstood the Texas lure just six years. In the fall of 1854, he loaded his young wife Eliza, his four small sons (the eldest, William, was just six years old), and their belongings into one four-horse wagon, ferried across the Red River, and reached the farthest extent of white settlement into the Indian frontier, in what is now Palo Pinto County, early in 1855.

But the Indians drove off the white man's cattle and horses, burned the white man's houses and haystacks, murdered the menfolk, and carried off the white women and children into captivity. As a defensive measure Captain Jack organized a frontier Texas Ranger Company and won fame as an Indian fighter.

Throughout his life he lived dangerously, but as the dark

93

clouds of civil war gathered over the country and men left the frontier to serve in the army, the Indian attacks forced the settlers to withdraw farther and farther eastward. By 1865, Captain Jack found it necessary to move his family (now increased to six children) to the southeast corner of Bosque County for greater security, while he remained one of the few men defending the frontier.

The war ended. The men came back. Adventure called again. In the spring of 1870, Captain Jack sold his home and farm, and with "twelve hundred cattle, seventy-six people, consisting of ten families, ten cowboys, twenty-nine vehicles all drawn by oxen" he led an expedition to California—his third such trip. He bought an irrigated farm near San Bernardino, but Texas was in his blood, and in just two years he sold out. Again the long wagon train inched across the mountains and deserts toward the tall prairie grasses of Bosque County.

In 1873, Captain Jack purchased the Sebastian Klippert Survey of one section near the northwest boundary of Bosque County and bordering on East Bosque Creek. This Survey had been granted in the form of the right to locate and have patented a given number of acres of land (land scrip) by reason of service in the Revolutionary War or early settlement within Texas. The right on scrip had been traded several times, and was finally patented to Caleb M. Hubby, a famous early land speculator in Texas. The first purchaser of the land (1870) had been George Lamon, who built a cabin near the creek bank and whose infant child is buried in an unmarked grave on the land.

As a neighbor on the south, Captain Jack enjoyed the

company of Colonel Buck Barry, equally famous as Indian fighter and Texas Ranger. Captain Jack was elected sheriff of Bosque County and made his ranch home his office.

The ranch on the East Bosque was a little paradise to Captain Jack, who never again left it. Today, with his wife, he lies buried in a little iron-fenced cemetery on a low hill overlooking his beloved prairie. Numerous ever running springs fed the little streams which joined to form East Bosque Creek. In dry times and wet, the sparkling water flowed beneath its canopy of overlocking tree branches to furnish water for the cattle and horses and other animals. Within its clear depth, fish darted, and on its surface, wild ducks and other waterfowl floated and sought their food.

From the river to the tops of the gentle hills lay sun-drenched acres of swaying grasses, six to eight feet high in the lowlands, dropping to two to four feet on the rocky outcrops. The soil was prodigiously fertile; the trees along the river furnished wood for buildings, corrals, and fuel; and wildlife was abundant—squirrel and rabbit, deer and antelope, coon, panther, wolf and coyote, quail and wild turkey, and tens of thousands of prairie chickens. Here was plentiful food and shelter for man and beast as Captain Jack had remembered it twenty-five years before when he had been mustered out of San Antonio. True, there were times when the droughts came, and the copper sun seared the rocks on Flat Top Mountain, and the grasses reached deeply into the earth for moisture. And sometimes in winter the ice storms came and the animals sought shelter in the tall matted grass or in the trees along the river.

Captain Jack selected a beautiful site for his home near

the edge of a break, standing about seventy-five feet above the river. Here he built a T-shaped box house with roomy comfortable porches. At the corner of the house, he dug a well to supply the family with cool, pure water, and down the slope to the east, he put up the necessary barn and corrals for his animals. On a well-drained gentle slope beyond the barn, he planted a fine orchard of peach and apple trees, and at the bottom of the slope, on rich subirrigated land, he laid out his garden. The land was so wondrously fertile that anything would grow, and he supplied his family with fine vegetables of all kinds, as well as blackberries, melons, and other small fruits.

Among the tall grasses along the river were open stands of pecan trees with interspersed oaks and elms forming open savannah. The bluestem and Indiangrass were well established and had a root system so heavy that clearing for a field was a difficult task. But with two yoke of oxen and a single twelve-inch moldboard plow, he struggled to overturn the thick, rich, black sod, the product of centuries of soil building. Eventually ninety acres were cleared, and this was considered the best field along the whole of the East Bosque. Here he grew bounteous crops of corn and sorghum. The corn was fed to his animals or ground for family use. An old horse or mule, treading round and round, pressed the juice from the sorghum in a little mill near the house. When the juice was boiled down thick and syrupy, it formed the principal sweetening for the table or cooking.

The steep, rocky break between the field and the prairie was covered with grass, and at the top, seemingly growing on the hardest of rocks, were several venerable live oak

96

trees that shaded the house. No cedars grew on the break, or on the undulating prairie stretching for miles in all directions from the escarpment.

To protect his corn from the cattle that fed on the open range, Captain Jack built a fence where the field adjoined the break. Long before barbed wire came into general use, rock served for fence material because the few trees found along the rivers were needed for houses and fuel and other purposes. So proficient was Captain Jack in laying the stones and chinking them just right that he was in charge of the construction of miles of rock fences built in the East Bosque area. Those fences still stand today wherever they have not been deliberately destroyed.

All livestock roamed the open range, and Captain Jack's Longhorns had all of the present Flat Top Ranch for their pasture. Shortly before his death in 1881, Captain Jack, as did most of his neighbors, turned to sheep raising. The Texas Central Railway had been constructed through his land, with Walnut Springs established as a switch. From there, wool was shipped by the freight-train load to Funston Brothers in St. Louis.

With the death of Captain Jack, the land passed into the possession of his eldest son, William E. Cureton, who later became a member of the Texas legislature. Here William's family was born, and one of his sons, Calvin Mapes Cureton, served as chief justice of the Texas Supreme Court for nearly twenty years, from 1921 to 1940.

Because of his duties in Austin, the new owner did not live all the time on the ranch. But whether in Austin or in Walnut Springs, the Cureton family looked upon the land as a precious heritage to be cared for so that it might produce food for a thousand generations to come. The fields were kept free of gulleys or encroaching vegetation. The ranges were never overstocked, and each year the grasses grew waist high and made their seeds.

By 1885, as more and more families moved into the Bosque Country bringing more and more cattle and sheep, it became necessary to fence the ranges as well as the cultivated fields. The thin-shanked Texas Longhorn had been a useful animal when one of its most important characteristics had to be fleetness of foot to escape wolves and other predators. But the markets of the East demanded better beef, and producing animals for choice juicy steaks required improved breeding. The day of the barbed wire and the windmill had come to Texas. After fencing, many ranchers began to graze their grass too heavily, but the Cureton place was kept in a high state of productivity until it was sold to Teel Ownbey in 1907.

Mr. Ownbey was a good farmer, but not a very good financier. He had eight children, and they obtained all of their living from the land. The river-bottom soil was still very fertile, and it produced corn and cotton as cash crops, as well as fruit in abundance for the family. Soon after purchasing the land, he broke out eighty-five acres of upland prairie to raise additional feed for his cattle. This soil was rich and fertile, as it had been developed under a thick cover of tall grasses. About the same time, a small house, barn, and well were constructed near the new fields to be occupied by a daughter and her family. Mr. Ownbey always lived in the house near the river.

The Reclamation of the Cureton Place

As he grew older, it became increasingly difficult for him to carry on the work of the farm. Eventually he became crippled and had to walk with a crutch. Very subtly, changes began to take place. The bottom field could not be so carefully cultivated, and two big gullies started. Trees and brush and tangled vines slowly encroached from the river, and a few trees appeared in the fence row. Cedars, live oaks, red oaks, and other timber commenced to grow on the breaks and invade the pastures here and there, where the grasses were weakening from overgrazing. It had all come about so slowly it had hardly been noticed.

In 1938, Mr. Pettit bought the adjoining land and wished to construct a good fence between his property and that of his neighbor. He discussed the fence with Mr. Ownbey, who consented to have the post holes dug as his share of the expense. A few days later Mr. Pettit found Mr. Ownbey hobbling on his crutch trying to dig the holes himself. The fence was completed at Flat Top expense, post holes and all. There is deep appreciation for a neighbor who makes so sincere an effort to carry out his bargain. Mr. Ownbey was a very good man.

After 1938, the land deteriorated rapidly. Efforts at producing crops were failures, which forced the livestock to live on the range without any supplemental feed. There had never been income enough to purchase modern machinery and tractors, so the one-row plows and other meager pieces of farm equipment were horse drawn. There were always from eight to twelve head of scrawny work animals, and they added their need to the already overburdened range. Very quickly the tall grasses were eaten off, and a

99

heavy stand of weeds took their place. Someone suggested that sheep would devour the weeds, so sheep were added to the dying range without cutting down on the number of cattle and horses. The climax grasses almost disappeared. The poorer grasses remaining were too weak to resist the invading weeds and cactus, cedar and sumac, scrub oak and elm, which spread a thick cover over the once productive prairie.

The land, which had been in cultivation more than twenty-five years, deteriorated also. Continuous cropping of corn, cotton, and small grains, without the addition of fertilizer or legumes, brought the inevitable result. The soil structure broke down, yields declined, weeds crept in, the once rich topsoil washed from the unprotected land in thin layers year after year, and gullies began forming in the old plow furrows.

The field in the once rich bottom land also slowly sank into decadence. After nearly seventy years of continuous planting to corn and cotton with no soil-building crops, fertility declined to the point where it was hardly worth while to plant seed. The tangle of trees and vines and shrubby growth pushed more rapidly into the neglected field from the river. Trees along the fence rows increased. Great branches extended twenty-five feet out over the field, and multitudes of small trees grew under the larger ones, many of them slanting at an angle of as much as forty-five degrees toward the sun.

A ditch had been built across the field to carry surplus water from three hundred acres of prairie, which lay above the break, some fifty to seventy-five feet higher than the bottom land. This ditch became choked with silt from the eroding land above, until it stood several feet higher than the rest of the field, and trees and matted underbrush grew rank and unimpeded along its course. Near the lower end of the original ditch, there was an overfall of seven or eight feet eating its way back into the field. The two gullies had continued to grow, deepening and widening with each rain and extending numerous fingers into the good bottom land on either side.

No roads connected the fields with the house or led to the public highway. Only a series of eroded ruts showed where narrow-tired wagons and buggies had made tracks during wet weather between the house and a rusted wire gate which led into another man's property.

In the little cemetery on the gentle hill, Captain Jack's monument stood in the midst of desolation and ruin where once there had been a paradise. So many farms and ranches have gone through the same cycle and been abandoned, turning vast stretches of the tall grass prairie of Central Texas into a worthless area of cedar, mesquite, cactus, and eroding denuded land.

But it does not have to be like that. The difference between prosperity and starvation is management. Under good management, the tall grasses can be made to grow again. This was the belief of Flat Top's owner as he sorrowfully observed his neighbor's land from the grassy pasture he had restored to its original lush growth on his side of the fence.

In 1948, he bought the run-down farm that had been Captain Jack's paradise. It was incomprehensible to his neighbors why anyone should spend so much as a dime on a piece of land that looked so forlornly hopeless.

But the task of reclamation was begun. The tumbledown buildings were all removed, and the decrepit and rusted machinery carted off for junk, including an ancient threshing machine, reminiscent of better days. Roads were constructed to make access easy, and the broken-down fences demolished.

The best land on most farms in the area is bottom land. There nature has cached the accumulated richness of thousands of years of soil building. And because it was the best, and would yield the greatest and most immediate returns for the investment of money and labor, the work of restoration was centered here.

But the condition of the ninety-acre field of river bottom land was almost unbelievable. Only a man with a deep faith in the abiding permanence of agriculture could see a future in so hopeless a place.

Before the land could be plowed and the soil building program begun, it had to be cleared and leveled. The low-branching limbs of the huge trees that had grown on the fence rows and along the river bank made it impossible to get machinery onto the land. Four men with axes, working from the deck of a truck for an entire day, barely made clearance for the tractor. During June of that year, one rain had dumped four inches of water on the high prairie which drained across the field. Logs had been washed down from the wooded break and lodged in the field, and some were so large they had to be removed with a tractor. The old ditch was cleared of trees and brush and leveled. The sides of the two big gullies and the overfall were bulldozed in.

But clearing and leveling were not all that had to be done. Changes were made in the field boundaries as well. Along the river, many small spots, grown up to trees and sprouts, were cleaned out, to add more land to the cultivated area. An old fence, separating this field from that of a neighbor, had grown up with large hackberry trees. Nothing could be salvaged here, so the trees were removed, the old fence torn down, and a new and substantial one built.

But it was on the side of the field toward the break that the greatest change took place. The water still drained off the three-hundred-acre upper prairie, and, with the elimination of the waterway across the bottom field, a diversion ditch had to be built. Flat Top Ranch has long been a co-operator with the Bosque Soil Conservation District, so the local work unit technician was called in. Since a service road was needed, the ditch was laid out with a broad, flat bottom and a levee wide enough for a gravel all-weather road, which serves the field and the adjoining range areas. The field is protected, and the nearly level waterway, which was soon covered with native grasses and King Ranch bluestem, is used as an auxiliary pasture. The changing of the field boundaries reduced the amount of land in the field, and most of that taken out of cultivation was sloping.

The summer of 1948 had been hot and very dry, so the corn crop, planted by the previous owner, yielded only a pathetic little ten bushels to the acre. Less than a mile and a half up the East Bosque, on a restored field of the Flat Top Ranch, the tall, sturdy plants produced fifty bushels.

103

The old field needed much care and good conservation medicine.

As soon as it was cleared and leveled and the corn removed, a soil-building crop was planted. Rye and nitrogen-building vetch, planted together in the fall for winter growth, following a generous application of superphosphate, made an excellent tonic for the sick land. The plants made only a fair growth. Purple-flowered vetch did not develop into large vines, nor did the rye make more than medium growth, in spite of the wet winter and spring. But recovery had begun. During the late spring months, a few cattle grazed until the plants became dormant. Then the remaining growth was plowed under to enrich the soil, and the land was given the rest cure until time for fall plowing.

Superphosphate was again added to the soil, and the same crops were planted. The fall and winter rains were generous, and the rye and vetch came up quickly and made vigorous growth. The land responded well. So well, in fact, that the field furnished winter grazing to a herd of cattle until the middle of April (1950). When the livestock were removed, the plants grew lustily until they were plowed under about the last of May.

Again the rest cure was applied, and by fall the field was ready for other crops. On thirty-five acres, a very large amount of superphosphate was worked into the soil, and alfalfa was planted. The remainder of the field was seeded to oats. Although the fall and winter of 1950–51 were very dry, the oats made fair growth, and the alfalfa did surprisingly well.

The long drought, which began in the fall of 1950, slowed

This fine bluestem grass provided the quality and quantity of feed necessary for these fine Hereford heifers.

Flat Top cows at one of the many reservoirs on the ranch.

the recovery of this field, but at no time stopped it. Each year, the soil grew more fertile, and its water-holding capacity increased as more and more organic matter was added. Every winter, vetch with either barley or rye was planted on parts of the field not in alfalfa. During the growing season, livestock grazed it, or in lieu of this, bales of alfalfa hay were put up and hauled away and stored in the barns for winter use.

By the spring of 1952, less than four years after the improvement program began, the field was again ready for a corn crop. This was a very dry year, and all the corn was used for silage. The remarkable thing was that the part of the field that had been in barley and vetch already yielded more than the average for corn in the community. But the real surprise came from the section of the field that had been in alfalfa for two years. Here the corn yield was twice that of the barley and vetch section—an amazing demonstration of the soil building qualities of alfalfa!

Oats followed corn the next year, 1953. In spite of drought conditions, this field yielded seventy-five bushels to the acre, while the average in the community was only thirty-five bushels. The old field had now recovered its strength and vigor, and was approaching the productivity of the virgin soils of sixty years before.

Six baby deer were found hidden in this cool oat field near the river when a crew was cutting the crop with a wind-rowing machine. Wildlife forms an essential part of the balance of nature maintained on the Flat Top Ranch, and shelter, food, and water are shared by the many deer, antelope, foxes, rabbits, squirrels, quail, turkey, geese, and other wild creatures, even though—as in the oat field that year—an antler now and then punctures the tire of a tractor.

Drought continued to sear the fields and pastures of Texas through 1954. The oat yield was only thirty bushels to the acre—but most fields in the neighborhood were not even harvested. In July, the whole field was plowed with a subsoiler to a depth of twenty-four inches to further open up the soil, improve its structure, and add to its ability to absorb water. With this treatment, crops will be still further increased.

One thing more has been added: In March of 1955, pipe was placed underground to form a complete irrigation system from the water of the creek. That time in March marked four and one-half years of very severe drought, yet the soil was moist from the top to the bottom of the three foot ditches dug to place the pipe. Alfalfa had been planted the October before, and the men were astonished to find the roots down twenty-four inches in the cool, damp ground. Now drought can never menace this field so long as the East Bosque flows—and the water-conservation program on the ranch means permanent protection to the river. Bumper crops of alfalfa can be grown, with two tons to the acre per cutting and four to five cuttings a year—or other crops in equal abundance.

What has been done to restore this rich bottom land to its original fertility is simple and can be done by anyone— and the rewards will pay the cost many times over in the long years and centuries that the field may be used if it is properly cared for—a permanent field on a permanent ranch.

The beat-up range had only remnants of the better

grasses left. After careful consideration, the decision was made to fence it off and close it to grazing for at least three years, in the hope that some recovery could be made in that length of time. Brush and trees also were removed.

Even under the severe drought conditions of the following years, range improvement was continuous. After only one year of deferment, the range was ready for moderate grazing, which has continued throughout the dry years. Sideoats grama was the first plant to show up in abundance, followed by little bluestem. As the range conditions improve, more productive Indiangrass and big bluestem will eventually make up part of the cover.

Even under drought conditions, the old Cureton place has recovered. Once more the tall grasses have spread over the rolling hills. The cedars and the cactus are gone, and the weeds are thinning out under competition from vigorous grass.

What has been done on the old Cureton place can be done on a multitude of other run-down Texas acres. It might require more time than in this case, but to the man who plans for the land to provide food for him and his children and his children's children for generations to come, the cost is small when compared with the benefits to be obtained.

Chapter 9

"DEDICATED TO THE IMPROVEMENT OF HEREFORDS"

W. B. ROBERTS

YEARS AGO THE present owner of Flat Top Ranch and his father tried various breeds commercially on their ranch in Archer County, Texas. Their decision to retain Herefords was no snap decision, but was based on the fact that year in and year out, through good conditions and bad, the Herefords gave them the best income. They had seen other breeds come and go, but the popularity of Herefords increased in the ranching country.

The successful experiences of early cattlemen proved that it was very important to wean a large calf crop percentage —to have good weight on these cattle when marketed—and to be able to do it even under drought conditions. Mr. Pettit readily admits that the Hereford did not prove to be perfect, but he emphasizes that it is easy to become blinded until "one cannot see the forest for the trees." It is the superior beef-making qualities, and not the minor faults, which explain why 81 per cent of the beef cattle today are Herefords.

During fourteen years of close association, the writer heard the reasons recited why whitefaces stayed in spite of many trying conditions. These reasons were brought out and dusted off whenever it looked as if other beef breeds were gaining in favor and when a major controversy brewed within Hereford circles.

Therefore, when Mr. Pettit purchased Flat Top Ranch in 1938, it was only natural that he should buy Herefords. Recent research confirmed what the Pettits had learned earlier from experience. California Agricultural Experiment Station *Bulletin No. 745*, released in September, 1954, gives the results of one of the tests.

One hundred and one Hereford cows were placed in a pasture by themselves. From March to September of 1947, two Hereford and two Brahman bulls were placed simultaneously in the pasture with these cows. The 1948 calf crop resulting from these four bulls running with the 101 cows totaled 93 head. Of the total calf crop, 57 were straight Hereford and only 36 were Brahman-Hereford.

During the 1948 breeding season, two Shorthorn bulls were also placed with the 101 Hereford cows along with, and at the same time as, the two Hereford bulls and the two Brahman bulls. In 1949, these cows produced a 100 per cent calf crop. However, with equal breeding opportunities for all the bulls, the resultant calf crop was 44 straight Herefords, 31 Brahman-Herefords and 26 Shorthorn-Herefords.

For the 1949 breeding season, 99 cows were used and the same plan of using six bulls, two each of the same three breeds was followed. The 1950 calf crop totaled 83, of which 42, over 50 per cent, were straight Herefords, 25 Brahman-Hereford and 16 Shorthorn-Hereford.

The results of this test confirm the observations of these

109

practical Archer County cow men—the Hereford bulls were more aggressive and active.

The test was carried even further, and weaning weights for the first and third year calves were determined. The first calf crop, resulting from the use of Hereford and Brahman bulls on the Hereford cows, had the following weaning weights: Hereford steer calves, 452 pounds; Brahman-Hereford steer calves, 423 pounds; Hereford heifer calves, 438 pounds; Brahman-Hereford heifer calves, 430 pounds. For the final year, 1950, the Hereford steer calves weighed 434 pounds; Brahman-Hereford steer calves, 413 pounds; Shorthorn-Hereford steer calves, 413 pounds; Hereford heifer calves, 389 pounds; Brahman-Hereford heifer calves, 395 pounds; and Shorthorn-Hereford heifer calves, 360 pounds.

These same calves were carried through a feeding test and the Herefords were superior.

Mr. Pettit's initial investment was a herd of polled Herefords. After that, he bought entire herds of horned Herefords as they were offered for sale. The best animals were retained as foundation stock. He noticed, after spending much time in the pastures with his cattle, that his horned Herefords outweighed and outgained his polled Herefords consistently, so the muleys were eliminated. His first experience had been entirely with commercial cattle, but he became interested in purebreds and began studying the literature about them. Then, as now, the only information in book form dealt with straight *Anxiety 4th* breeding. As his interest grew, he hired a college student during vacation to determine the percentage of *Anxiety 4th* blood in each of his cattle. After this was determined, they were divided into three groups, and each was given a separate horn brand. Animals carrying less than 10 per cent *Anxiety 4th* blood were horn branded zero, those in the 10 to 17.5 per cent bracket were horn branded two, and all those above 17.5 carried a three on their horns. At this time and for several years after, Mr. Pettit spent a great deal of his time on horseback, which enabled him to make sound plans for developing the ranch and improving his cattle program. From observations made on these horseback rides he noticed that the least intensely bred animals were the most thrifty under range conditions.

On account of a drop in cattle prices, many herds were offered for sale. Mr. Pettit bought several of these herds, and after selecting the top individuals, the remainder were sold. Also, about this same time, a select group of grade Herefords were chosen from the A. K. Harky herd in Menard County as foundation stock for a commercial herd. After comparing the performance of these later groups with that of the intensely bred *Anxiety 4th* group, it was obvious the "outcross" cattle were hardier and thriftier under strictly range conditions at Flat Top.

The needs of the commercial breeder set the pattern at Flat Top, and emphasis has been placed on the practical kind of a Hereford rather than on the show-ring type.

At this stage in Flat Top's development, Hereford breeders were turning more and more to a smaller or comprest type of animal. This was brought on because of stiff competition in steer classes with other breeds competing for honors at livestock shows. Battle lines had formed, and

111

many breeders of long standing who had bred the practical, "natural" animal for many years thought it necessary to get on the "band wagon." It looked, read, and sounded as if all Hereford breeders would have to breed the smaller, compact animal in order to be popular and to make a profit.

"I am not sure whether I have found a rope or lost a calf." This remark was made by Mr. Pettit to a group from the National Hereford Breeders Association gathered in the ranch sale pavilion. The group had just come from the National Hereford Congress held in Fort Worth, where the main discussion theme, led by Dr. A. D. Weber of Kansas State College, had been to encourage breeders to strive for more size in Hereford cattle. For several years prior to this National Congress, there had been a great deal of concern and discussion among Hereford breeders relative to the small size toward which the breed was gradually being headed. From Mr. Pettit's early experiences with his father on a ranch in West Texas, he was convinced there should be no great disagreement among purebred breeders on this point. He remembered that the roomier cows and bulls were the ones that paid the bills. So the big ones stayed.

The highly regarded secretary of the American Hereford Association, R. J. Kinzer, was very much opposed to the new fad for comprest cattle. Mr. Pettit leaned on him greatly for help in choosing his first cattle. His influence was due in great part to the inspiration he was able to impart to anyone working for the improvement of the Hereford breed.

The writer showed cattle at the various state and national shows during R. J.'s tenure in office. It was not unusual to see him helping the herdsmen shake up straw for bedding before the Herefords arrived at the show. Many times he would meet the train and help lead those "precious Herefords" to the show barn, even in late hours of the night, and he would be one of the first on the job in the morning. Little wonder that his advice was so helpful—he had had a lifetime of experience from the ground up, and, best of all, he had a big heart to go with his knowledge.

Another important factor which prevented an abrupt switch to the trend for comprest types of cattle was the fact that the ranch's commercial bull customers were staying "old fashioned." To us at Flat Top, the preference of the commercial bull buyer sets the pattern we follow. As purebred breeders, we have the responsibility for furnishing him bulls which will produce beef more efficiently and economically.

The wisdom of the decision to avoid the popular trend of that period is now being borne out experimentally. Eight years of results from New Mexico A. & M. College experiments show that in weight-for-age selections, large Hereford cows (long legs and body) hold the edge over compact cows of the same breed. John Knox, head of the New Mexico A. & M. Animal Husbandry Department, says that the study indicates that large cows stay in the herd almost a year longer than the compact type. In calving percentage, the larger cows best the others by 10 per cent, with a 96.5 per cent calving record.

This advantage continues at weaning time—93.8 per cent calves weaned from large cows, compared with only 81.6 per cent from the smaller, compact animals.

113

On a herd lifetime average, the large cows produced one and one-half more calves. Average weight of calves from large cows was one hundred pounds more than calves from compact cows.

When the calving figures are interpreted on the basis of average calf weight for each one thousand pounds of cow in the herd, the advantage for the large cows is still forty-seven pounds more calf output per animal. Also calves from larger cows show the highest average daily gain.

During the course of the experiment more than twenty lots of steers were marketed. It was a tossup between compact and large cows as far as carcass grade of their calves could be determined. Big cows eat more, but only in direct proportion to the difference in body weights between large and compact cattle, the test shows.

Herds of purebred cattle purchased early in the history of Flat Top were bought from Robt. L. Cook of Jourdantown, Texas; Milton Kasch, San Marcos, Texas; W. H. Goldsmith, Cleburne, Texas; Tom Parrott Estate, Throckmorton, Texas; and George Drewry of Dallas, Texas. While a few outstanding individuals from these herds were to play a part in the original foundation, a later purchase of the entire Elliott Roosevelt herd furnished a herd bull and a number of cows which were to have far-reaching effects on the future of the Flat Top herd and Hereford breed. With this purchase came *HT Mischief Tone,* who was to sire the outstanding show winners *CP Tone, Carlos Tonette,* and *Flat Top Flossie.* The grand champion carload of bulls in the 1942 Fort Worth livestock show were predominantly sons of this outstanding herd sire. *C.P. Tone* sired the outstanding heifer *Dominette of CP*. While these cows were purchased from Elliott Roosevelt, they had been bred by well-known Hereford breeders, John and Horace Sedwick of Albany, Texas. These large cows were of *"The Mischief"* breeding and were of the kind which we need more of at this time. Under pasture conditions, they would get extremely fat when dry, but would milk down thin after calving. All of the cows of this breeding were dark. This fact is contrary to the rather widespread opinion that easy fleshing qualities are associated with light or "yellow" color.

The bull in service, *HT Mischief Tone*, was bred by the Harper and Turner Ranch and was a combination of four popular lines of breeding—*Hazlett, Prince Domino, Bonnie Brae*, and *Mischief Mixer*. At maturity he weighed about a ton and was powerfully built. Besides being an excellent calf-getter, he had unusual powers of reasoning, which were observed by the writer when he first came to the ranch. At that time, it was the practice to turn all the herd bulls together at the end of the breeding season. Of course a battle royal resulted for a few days, but they finally calmed down. *Mischief Tone* would stay off to one side by himself and take no part unless another bull forced the fight. Then he would push heads with his adversary till he got in position to slide his head up and use his right horn like a trip hammer. He had horns which came out from his head about eight inches, and he had learned to use the right horn for the knockout punches. After about three blows the other bull would bellow and run off. The writer's belief in the intelligence of this bull was further strengthened by observing his actions during natural service—if it were a mature cow, he completed his job with all speed, but with the heifers and nervous younger cows he was easy and gentle.

The "old" bull's value was appreciated, and to get maximum service from him, we frequently bred him to three cows in one day. Although it was not common practice and not recommended, it was necessary one day to put three cows which were to be bred in the lot with him simultaneously. In his slow, powerful strides he served one cow after another and retired to a corner of the lot without showing a second interest in any one of them.

Shortly after the Sedwick purchase, another important addition to the foundation herd was obtained from the F. W. Alexander herd at Albany, Texas. Twenty daughters of *Victor Domino and Diamond* were in this draft. Although these cows were very old when purchased, they were all carrying the service of the outstanding herd sire *Beau Gwen 50th*. This bull had been champion bull at the Fort Worth Livestock Show as a junior bull calf, and history has since proved he added much improvement to the Hereford breed. He was a large, light-colored bull with an unusually heavy loin and hind quarter. Little did we know at the time that fifteen years later it would be one of the most sought-after bloodlines. In addition to fine quality, these cattle had another very desirable characteristic—longevity. In fact, this group of cows added so much improvement that the owner of Flat Top went back in 1943 and paid F. W. Alexander $1,750 each to select the top twenty cows out of his Diamond Ranch herd. With the exception of one, a daughter of *Victor Domino,* they were all daughters of *Beau Gwen 50th.*

116

"Dedicated to the Improvement of Herefords"

In the Alexander dispersion of May, 1945, there was another opportunity to add more of this blood. By this time, a cross of *Real Prince Domino* blood had been added through the bull *Real Prince Domino 112*. Like *Beau Gwen 50th,* he was a light-colored bull weighing about 2,100 pounds, and had a strong loin and hind quarter. Of the thirty-nine head which were purchased at this time, many still are working in the herd.

Only one other group of cattle has contributed greater numbers to the foundation of the Flat Top herd than the *Beau Gwen 50th* group. That group was suggested by the former secretary of the American Hereford Association, R. J. Kinzer, and came from Willow Creek Ranch (Stephenson and Hoover, owners) at Belt, Montana. When one of the partners, Mr. Stephenson, died in 1942, it was necessary to sell some of the cattle to settle the estate. Mr. Pettit met Mr. Kinzer at Willow Creek. They selected thirty top cows and forty-five yearling heifers. There was much conjecture as to the wisdom of moving these cattle from the state of Montana to Texas. They were moved in the fall, by rail, and, notwithstanding the trip of ten days' duration, they arrived in good condition and suffered no subsequent setback from their journey.

The predominant bloodline represented in this Montana purchase was *Prince Domino 9th,* considered in R. J.'s careful judgment to be one of the four top sons of *Prince Domino*. He was owned in partnership by Willow Creek and Arthur Crawford-Frost of Alberta, Canada. In the Willow Creek herd, the bull had been crossed primarily on cows of *Beau Blanchard, Beau Mischief,* and *Beau Randolph*

117

breeding. These cows were very similar to the *Beau Gwen 50th* cattle in that they were light colored and had plenty of scale. They were grown, like the *Beau Gwen 50th* cattle, on the range rather than in the feedlot. This was one of Mr. Pettit's strict requirements, as he was confident, then as now, that economical production of cattle is dependent on the kind of breeding that will produce efficiently on pasture. He subscribes to the old saying, "Breed is no stronger than pasture," and works day and night to improve both.

Although there are many good descendants of the *Prince Domino 9th* strain in the present herd of matrons, the three which are most widely known are *Martha Mischief J,* champion at Denver in 1946; *Carlos Tonette,* champion at many state fairs and a class winner at Denver; and *Flat Top Flossie,* champion at many of the larger shows. They in turn are contributing to the improvement of the herd—*Martha,* with a grandson; *Carlos,* a son; and *Flossie,* two daughters.

So well did this group of females fit the demands of the ranch's breeding program that when a dispersion of the Willow Creek herd was necessitated by Mr. W. H. Hoover's death ten years later, the fifty top females were selected from there to be added to those already at Flat Top. Mr. Hoover had visited Flat Top, and he and the owner of Flat Top had become good friends. He appreciated Mr. Pettit's efforts to improve Herefords so much that he had instructed the executor of his estate on his death to give Flat Top first choice of the females in the herd.

Two other smaller, but important, groups of cattle were added with a specific purpose in mind.

Mr. Pettit had long been mindful of the serious breeding

program conducted by the Hazletts of Kansas, whose cattle excelled both in the pasture and in the show-ring. He had a desire to infuse some, but not too much, Hazlett blood into his herd. He wanted a little of this blood because of beefiness and easy feeding characteristics of the animals, but not too much—because the milking qualities were not up to Flat Top standards. Again R. J. came to the rescue with a top selection of Hazlett breeding from the herd of Frank Robert Condell. Seven of the twelve selected were daughters of the well-known *Hazford Rupert 71st.*

The other group of fifteen bred heifers was selected from the herd of Mr. Crawford-Frost of Alberta, Canada, by Mr. Cal Kinzer. One died before delivery, and a second was not allowed to cross the border because of an inverted tattoo. This Alberta herd was notorious for producing some of the best large Herefords on the continent. The bull mostly responsible for this record was *Silver Standard.* On many occasions he had sired the champion bull or winning group at the 800- to 1,000-head bull sale held each year in Calgary. The breeding back of *Silver Standard* is *Real Prince Domino* on the sire's side and *Prince Domino 9th* on the dam's side, both good bloodlines.

By this time, the reader may have concluded that after so many different groups of breeding had been assembled, that herd uniformity would be absent. But this was not the case because Flat Top's owner found the field for selection wide enough that he chose the type of animals he wanted in most bloodlines examined. When selecting for his foundation herd, he had a basic type in mind—not type in terms of a fitted animal, but in terms of the utility or range animal.

119

The best cows in the country cannot continue to improve the breed without a better bull or bulls to mate them to. The cow will not influence the quality of over seven or eight calves in her life, but in his lifetime, a bull may affect the quality of 150 to 1,000 calves, depending on the breeding method used. At the time the Flat Top herd was being assembled, the owner and the writer agreed that a general weakness of the breed was in the hindquarter. It was too short and too shallow, and the hind legs were crooked. Therefore we agreed that one goal would be to improve the quality of the hindquarter.

Secondly, we agreed we were in the registered Hereford business simply to provide bulls which would work improvements on commercial herds of beef cattle. To put the same statement in a different way, the goal is to produce a calf that will look good and weigh heavy at weaning time —the same calf to develop and look good and still weigh heavy at approximately eighteen months to two years.

Many purebred Hereford breeders who have visited and made purchases at Flat Top Ranch have made the statement that they were going back home and make a greater effort to produce better Herefords. A typical excerpt from a letter says, "After looking at these cattle I culled my cattle from 126 head down to the 40 best ones, and am starting out to see if I can produce some Herefords like yours."

It is flattering to produce bulls of quality good enough to go into the good Texas herds of O'Connor Brothers at Victoria; Hayes and Joe Mitchell, Ken and Tyrrel Smith, Marfa; Gage Estate, Eagle Pass; Halsell Cattle Company, San Antonio; Carter McGregor, Wichita Falls; J. T. Davis,

Prize Flat Top Hereford calves bedded in Texas Blue-bonnets.

Flat Top Pride, one of the better bulls of the Hereford breed.

"Dedicated to the Improvement of Herefords"

Sterling City; and about 150 bulls were selected by W. J. Gourley for his WS Ranch at Cimarron, New Mexico.

Other repeat Texas purchasers who have favored Flat Top with their business are W. A. Blackwell, Cuero; Moore Brothers, Navasota; Gus and Charles Schreiner, Kerrville; Palomas Ranch, Falfurrias; and Jack Love of Llano.

Fortunately we had started out with two good herd sires, *H. T. Mischief Tone* and his son, *CP Tone*. With the growth of the cow herd, it was necessary to add bull power. After much searching, we found a bull that fitted the pattern of the other two bulls. He had already been selected by Turner Ranch of Sulphur, Oklahoma, for use in their own herd. It took the highest price paid for a Hereford bull in twenty-two years to transfer *Beau Zento T 36th* to Flat Top. He was a dark-colored, 2,000-pound bull, with exceptional length and depth of quarter; length, width, and thickness of loin; desirable symmetry of lines; very straight legs; and a better than average head. He was very active, and carried himself on the walk like a ship sailing on the ocean. He lived up to his heritage in that he and his offspring were fast gainers under pasture conditions. The writer has not had experience with another bull of any breed that was as prolific as this one. As a result of hand breeding over a period of nine months, natural service, he sired a calf crop of 105 calves in the year 1945.

These statistics still stand out in the writer's mind for two reasons. First, it was unusual to get so many calves from one sire without using artificial insemination. Secondly, the writer had just employed a local lady for office help. Her first job was to determine the number of calves born in

121

proportion to the previous season's services of the respective herd bulls. When the list had been prepared and the report was being delivered orally, there was a pause after reading, "*Beau Zento T 36th—214* services," then the following, "That's not right, is it?"

Putting such a load on one bull is not considered judicious, but because of a serious injury to *CP Tone* which incapacitated him for the season, rather than use a less valuable bull, *Beau Zento's* duty was doubled.

Notwithstanding the fact that fitting cattle for show is a necessary evil and the best form of advertising, it has not become the primary purpose of breeding purebred Herefords at Flat Top. Generally, when a bull has been highly fitted, it shortens his breeding life and reduces his efficiency. Highly fitted heifers, with few exceptions, are difficult to get with calf, have difficulty calving, and do not furnish enough milk to feed their calves. When Flat Top adopted the motto, "*Dedicated to the Improvement of Herefords*," it was not meant to apply to a few show cattle but to the herd as a whole. This statement is so applicable that we did not know *Beau Zento's* calves had earned enough points in two seasons to list him among the Register of Merit sires until it appeared in the American Hereford Journal. Many of his daughters are in the cow herd, and two of his sons are carrying on where he left off.

Beau Zento's offspring are not only widespread in his homeland, but one of his sons went to the well-known Jorge Pereda herd in the Argentine, another was sold to Roger P. Jones, of Lloydminster, Alberta, Canada, and a third went to the Edward and Evelyn Rushmore herd in Southern Rhodesia. When the latter was loaded and flown from the airport on the ranch to his embarkation port at New Orleans, he became the first bull to travel by air.

After using *Beau Zento* extensively four years, and while he was at the height of his popularity, we allowed him to be sold in one of our auctions. He sold to the Claude Heard Ranch, in Beeville, Texas, for $50,000, and is probably the cheapest bull we ever sold.

Although some of our bulls were going into registered herds, most were being bought by commercial breeders. Their demands were for ample bone, ample size, good legs and feet, reasonably good heads by the present standards, and light colors. Judging from the comments of the various purchasers, we were filling the bill fairly well except for colors. The cow herd by long odds was predominantly light colored, but *HT Mischief Tone, CP Tone,* and *Beau Zento T 36th* were dark colored. The first two bulls sired about half light and half dark colors, with the last-named siring 90 per cent dark. Although most commercial breeders prefer light colors, our experience is in agreement with the findings as reported in a bulletin prepared at the United States Southern Great Plains Field Station, Woodward, Oklahoma.

Effects of color on gains were studied during the 4-year period, 1946 to 1949, by classifying all experimental steers as to light-red, intermediate-red, and dark-red color shades. Gains were then computed for each class. The study was made to answer frequent inquiries of stockmen as to the relative gain-

123

ing ability of light and dark color Hereford cattle. The average of 1,796 steers showed no significant difference in seasonal or yearlong gains of the different color types.

Once again we were looking for a bull of the same type and quality as the ones we were using, but one that would help the color problem. While we were visiting Harrisdale Farms and looking over that great cow herd with Dr. Harris, an outstanding "yellow" cow was spotted. She was a daughter of *The Prince Domino 30th,* a bull which has been used with good results not only at Harrisdale, but also by Bridwell Hereford Ranch, George Keith, and John R. Black. The writer discovered she had a yearling son which was being kept for a herd bull. He was a grandson of the favorably known and popular *Prince Domino Return.* He became the property of Flat Top Ranch under the name *HD Prince RD 18th* which was later changed to *Flat Top Return.*

Return contributed much to the improvement of the herd, especially to the quality of the coat and fleshing. One of his first offspring, known as *Flat Top,* was champion steer at Houston in 1947 and sold for $15,000.

The registered herd had now attained such size that we needed another top-quality bull. The owner, always careful to keep the pastures improving, sold the grade Herefords in order to spread the cattle thinner.

The herd had been built up by using only our top bulls until it was hard to tell where the registered cattle pasture ended and the grade pasture began. One of the highlights of the West Texas Hereford Tour that season (1955) was a group of steer calves still with their mothers at the W. R.

124

Watt Ranch at Throckmorton, Texas. "Billy Bob" volunteered the information that every one of those mothers was a descendant of the group of cows he purchased here. In the short time which commercial Herefords were at Flat Top, two carloads of steers were fitted and shown. Both won grand championships at the Houston show.

The Return's calves were coming up to expectations with one exception—they did not have enough bone. We found the bull which we thought would be helpful in correcting this shortcoming at Colvert Ranch, Mill Creek, Oklahoma. He was a triple *Dandy Domino 90th* bull, named *CR Chief Defender 15th*. He not only had ample bone but had a tremendous hindquarter and carried this width from end to end. Although his head was very masculine and muscular, it could have been shorter, with more curly hair on it. He was very light colored and sired light colors consistently.

Thus, in his turn, *CR Chief Defender 15th* made his contribution to the herd at Flat Top, just as had the other individual bulls and the family lines brought in before him. The term *"A Flat Top Bull"* has come to have a special meaning in Hereford circles—big, ample bone, strong hindquarters, masculine head, and the inherent ability to do well on the range. There is satisfaction in this acknowledgment of progress to date in "the improvement of Herefords" at Flat Top. However, the fatal disease, "self-satisfaction," has not set in and the Flat Top motto will remain the same.

Chapter 10

BREEDING AND FEEDING MANAGEMENT
W. B. ROBERTS

AT THE TIME the ranch was fully stocked, the practice of artificial insemination was gaining in use. Flat Top, with its 1,000 cows, was an ideal place to test the practice under ranching conditions. The idea was appealing because you could hurry the trend toward uniformity by getting so many more calves from one top bull. Your need for top herd bulls that are hard to get would be greatly reduced. And best of all, you could increase the number of high-quality market bulls for commercial breeders and also be able to furnish large numbers of bulls by one sire.

We planned for this new project and bought a half interest in the tried-and-proven *TT Proud Prince* from Moseley Hereford Ranch in Jackson Hole, Wyoming. He had been in service before in the Thornton Hereford Ranch herd at Gunnison, Colorado. He, like the other bulls used, weighed close to a ton, was deep bodied and extra-heavy boned, thick fleshed and smooth. He was long on quality. His coat was of medium color, and his hide could be picked up and folded to the very root of his tail. The head was broad and strong, and he had much the same "personality" as our own *Mischief Tone*.

The artificial insemination program was carried on four years and was discontinued when it became impractical to shuttle the aging *Proud Prince* from the high Jackson Hole, Wyoming, country to low-altitude Texas.

Experience finally proved artificial insemination to be a very expensive program on a ranch with the size and topography of Flat Top. For example, pastures had to be checked at least twice daily each breeding season. Since conception, generally, is higher when service is close to the end of estrus, the best practice is to pen the cows when they first come in heat and hold them for breeding as they go out of heat. These extra chores are tedious and expensive.

An accident to *Flat Top Pride*, a top son of *Beau Zento T 36*, proved that the program does have value. While serving a cow in a wet pasture, he slipped and fell, breaking a pelvic bone. He was an excellent patient and after four months of good nursing was able to walk again, but our veterinarian warned against letting him serve naturally. His valuable services are still being continued, and are made possible only by artificial insemination.

To date the ranch has been fortunate, for the herd has had no diseases of the reproductive organs.

Not all of the females, nor all of the prospective herd bulls, added to the herd were allowed to remain a part of it. About the biggest sin an animal can commit is to fail to make proper development under natural range conditions.

The owner of Flat Top entered the purebred cattle business with the opinion, founded on his grade cattle experience, that some cattle inherited the ability to convert pasture plants into beef more efficiently than others. He has found this to be just as true in the pedigreed business, but, with the blood lines recorded, a record is available to determine, to a reasonably accurate extent, those lines of breeding which most economically fulfill these requirements. There is a traditional belief that Hereford cattle are the best rustlers of beef breeds, but in order to preserve and protect that heritage, it is necessary to improve that characteristic.

There is nothing new in the statement that cattle are smart enough to search out in the pasture the plants most beneficial to them, but this fact is important in grassland management.

Many range improving practices can be carried out which go far toward providing these efficient grass-using animals with both the quantity and quality of forage required.

There is much food for thought in the following, written by range authority B. W. Allred in his book, *Practical Grassland Management*:

Livestock graze cafeteria style. They select the best-smelling and tastiest forage season by season. That fact accounts for a great deal of their behaviour.

A thorough knowledge of the grazing habits of animals is essential if the ranchman is to set up a successful forage management program. And the right kind of range management is a necessity if our national livestock appetite is to be satisfied permanently. We need to know every thing we can learn about the animal's harvesting and digestive apparatus.

Fortunately grazing animals are not as frivolous in selecting their diet as civilized man; they haven't developed a craving for faddish foods. When they can get it, they prefer palatable, nourishing forage that provides a balanced diet of proteins, carbohydrates, and minerals. Green grasses, cereal grains, and legumes—the most desirable forage plants—make up the greater part of the livestock diet, when available. The key to continuous growth and good fleshing of animals is keeping before them an adequate and varied bill-of-fare of green forage, year-round if possible. As it is, too many of the nation's livestock are on a growing and fattening ration only four to six months of the year. The other six to eight months are on a maintenance or starving ration.

Any forage shortage thwarts livestock in exercising their *inborn ability* to roam over the range selecting a palatable, nourishing diet. To produce at their best, livestock need to be able to graze cafeteria style—to select the best-smelling and tastiest forage as the seasons advance.

The owner of Flat Top Ranch appreciates the above statement, and has directed all effort, as speedily as the work will allow, toward making the ranch the ideal natural home for his Herefords.

A large part of an animal's life is spent in search of food or water. If the food is scarce or poor in quality, the animal "walks off," in this search, much of the gain it should add or retain. This is true also when the watering places are scarce or far apart.

Horned cattle in general, and horned Herefords in particular, graze in open formation. Generally, you will find them scattered over the pasture rather than grazing in bunches, hence they make more uniform use of the pasture. This is very helpful in the bunchgrass country. It is only natural for the cattle to graze the young and tender plants throughout the season. If only one area of a pasture is grazed in the spring, it becomes overused as the stock keep taking the new growth. Unless cattle graze uniformly, some areas are used too much and others too little. Often it becomes necessary to mow the ungrazed bunches.

When pastures are overgrazed, undesirable plants come in. The nutritious perennials die out, and the annual plants increase. Cattle get hungry enough to eat what is available —plants that have very little food value and that even may be poisonous. This increases management problems in several ways, including loss of animals by chronic bloat, loss of calves by miscarriage, and indirectly by a loss of health when they become susceptible to disease.

In addition to these problems, the insects, especially grasshoppers, thrive and multiply on the annual plants, whereas they decrease where the perennial grasses are abundant. Snails, which are the hosts for the liver fluke, do not appear in areas which are covered with the desirable grasses.

Guarding the pasture grasses and checking the welfare of the cattle require that someone be on the alert in all seasons, under all kinds of weather conditions, and at all times. When Mr. Pettit reports to some of us that a remote part of a pasture is not getting proper use, it makes us continually aware of his deep interest in the pasture management that he has emphasized since he first knew about cattle and pastures.

When one realizes that from twelve to fifteen gallons of water are needed daily for a cow, the desirability of its being readily available can be appreciated. Watering places need to be closely spaced in order to reduce the amount of livestock trailing between waterings, to save animal gain, and to save grass which would otherwise be trampled out along trails and near watering places.

Economy in production of beef cattle is certainly dependent upon satisfying the animal's appetite. However, a lot of other things have much to do with ability to gain. If they have to travel too far for their food or water, if they have to battle flies and insects, or if they have no protection against extreme heat or cold, they use up energy which should go to producing beef. Experiments have shown that the maintenance energy for a steer that is lying down for half a day is, other conditions being equal, less than that for one lying down only one-third of a day.

Also it has been proved that in very hot weather the temperature is 10 degrees cooler in green pasture than in a barren lot. The ground temperature—where an animal breathes when grazing—is 40 degrees cooler in lush grass than it is where there is little cover in the hot summer time. These may seem like small matters, but they all add up to have their effect on reaping the full measure of an animal's inherent ability to produce.

When officials of the Bureau of Entomology at Washington were first looking for a place to experiment with fly control using the little known chemical DDT, they found receptive co-operation at Flat Top. This work was started in 1944, under the supervision of Dr. Laake, and various formulations and methods of application were tried. The effective and harmless features were discovered and the product was released later for public use.

Until the droughty spring and summer of 1952, it ap-

131

peared that the plan to carry one thousand Flat Top brood cows and the increment would balance with the natural forage produced. With a total rainfall of 14.98 inches in 1951 and 18.13 in 1952, the drought began taking its toll in the pastures. In December of 1952, the herd was reduced four hundred head by an auction sale. However, with a rainfall of only 19.11 inches in 1953, the old native grasses were making very little regrowth, and no new plants were to be found. It was then that the decision was made to reduce the size of the herd again. This time, O'Connor Brothers at Victoria bought 650 of our best females—three years old and under. A great deal of effort and time had gone into building the herd, but when an extended drought moves in, it is always wiser to sell many animals which were planned for foundation material and save the grass. While it is difficult to acquire or breed the kind of cattle which one sets up as an ideal, it is even more difficult to bring back the native grasses after the turf is destroyed. To put it simpler, it is easier to recover the cattle than the grass.

It takes a lot of doing to get a superlative animal, and the writer is reminded of a conversation which took place at a time when Fred DeBerard of Kremling, Colorado, was visiting Flat Top. At that time, Mr. DeBerard had about eight hundred brood cows. A local cattleman asked him how many good calves he got a year. His reply was, "Sometimes ten." When asked how many outstanding calves he got each year, he paused briefly and replied, "Sometimes none." Thus it is in the cattle game.

Another 230 females were sold to WS Ranch Company of Cimarron, New Mexico, and this was fortunate, because only 13.71 inches of rain fell in 1954. This process of adjusting the rate of stocking left 350 brood cows and young cattle, amounting to approximately 800 head. From this time on, the plan has been to improve the quality and increase the numbers dependent on the weather and rate of grass improvement.

The drought, coming as it did, was something over which we had no control, but about this same time another problem was brought to public attention—that problem was "dwarfism," and something could be done about it.

It first came to the writer's attention when a breeder invited him to visit him and see "the bull calf he had been hoping for for years." By show-ring standards, point for point, this calf was the ultimate. Unfortunately, time proved the calf to be a dwarfish monstrosity.

Certain cattle, like certain people, carry the genes that occasionally produce dwarfed individuals. These dwarf genes are inherited, and cattlemen with a breeding herd loaded with them are in serious trouble because midget cattle are unproductive. In purebred herds, the problem is tragic because bull buyers want normal bulls to breed to their cows. The problem has always existed in a minor way, but with modern intensified breeding programs, dwarfism has increased alarmingly.

On my first visit to another breeder's place, he proudly showed me his recent purchase of three bred heifers. By the time I made the second visit, two of these heifers had produced dwarfish calves that had to stand under their mothers and reach up to nurse. Only after seeing two similar situations did the writer become inquisitive enough to

133

discover it was not a problem for Herefords only, but for other breeds as well. It looked like a serious problem, to be sure, until research proved that there were still certain bloodlines within the breed which could be depended on to be free of the dwarf-producing gene. Cattle carrying the genes of dwarfism could be traced through the herd registry and removed for slaughter to free the herd. Our experience definitely confirms what is claimed by research findings.

As stated previously, the cow herd—selections starting in 1938—is predominantly of *Beau Gwen 50th, Anxiety 4th, Hazlett, Prince Domino Return, Prince Domino 9th,* and *Dandy Domino 90th* breeding. It is not known at this time if these fortunate selections were governed by the attempt to take advantage of the owner's early cattle experiences in Archer County, or if it was the result of "more luck than management."

Much could be written about the various experiments— good and bad—to produce the most practical supplemental feed. The ultimate goal is to produce year-round grazing of green forage. Until that is reached, we have a winter feeding period from November 15 to March 15. Since our preferred calving time is from October 1 to March 30, it is important that the brood cow receive some supplement. In drought years, when the bluestems do not make much growth, twenty pounds of good alfalfa hay daily per head is preferred. In normal seasons, with a good carry-over of the native bluestems, aided by the rescuegrass and Texas wintergrass, one and one-half to three pounds of cottonseed cake daily per head is satisfactory. When there is extra bad weather with snow or freezing rain, cattle are given a good fill of good quality grass hay plus a treat of some cotton-seed cake.

In the summertime, especially in the months of July and August, supplemental grazing on sudangrass provides a high protein diet for our cattle and gives us an excellent opportunity to rest the native grass pastures.

"I believe that cattle should be fed all of the nourishing feed they can consume to create growth." These are the words of the Flat Top Owner. Where and when supplemental feeding is practiced, it is done to get maximum body development and growth. This is to promote and prolong the usefulness of the animal in the breeding herd.

The most important period of development is when the animal is making its most rapid growth as a calf and yearling. When the calves are still with their dams in the pasture, they are allowed access to self-feeders filled with a grain mixture of ten parts by weight of whole oats and one part shelled corn. In periods of extremely dry weather, when there is little green feed, 10 per cent small linseed pellets are added to the ration. The calves automatically adjust their consumption of the feed, depending on the amount and palatability of natural food available. When they are weaned, they are carried through the first winter on this same mixture, at the rate of eight pounds a day.

When animals are fitted for show or special sale purposes, it is necessary for them to put on excess condition. When this is done, we use a ration of equal parts by weight of "good quality" crimped oats, coarse cracked corn, wheat bran, and one-half part small linseed pellets. This ration is more palatable if dampened with molasses water. Also, this mixture can be made more fattening by increasing the corn content, or less fattening by increasing the amount of bran. When given a concentrated grain ration, the animal should be fed ample good quality grass or prairie hay—with a twice-a-week feeding of green alfalfa hay. A book could be written on ways and means of fitting the animal for show, and there are several methods of accomplishing that end. But most important, one must start with a prospect that is of the generally accepted show type and one born with the inherent ability to convert the feed into beef.

It has been apparent that our well-cared-for pastures have no mineral problem. Although much salt is consumed the year round, there has been very small consumption of various minerals experimented with. Steamed bone meal and salt, fed free choice, have proved adequate.

The chief mission of the purebred Hereford breeder is the improvement of beef cattle—produced at a minimum cost. Each breeder must choose a goal that fits his own needs the best.

These desired improvements include economy of production, early maturity, easy feeding, fertility, and conformation. It is the problem of the individual breeder to discover the best methods of selecting, mating, and developing to achieve these ends.

The Hereford breed has earned the right to be universally approved. There is virtue in different bloodlines and methods, but they do not need to be used to the exclusion of all others. *It is to the detriment of the breed to follow "fads and fancies," and we are treading on dangerous ground when we—by design or carelessness—create a breed within the breed.*

136

Chapter 11

THE HOG ENTERPRISE

CHARLES PETTIT

BEFORE 1954, I HAD never liked hogs. To be compared to a hog was a great insult, because, to me, a hog was the symbol of both greediness and filthiness. I had never dreamed of raising hogs until 1954, when Louis Bromfield made one of his frequent visits to the ranch. He gave me such an enthusiastic account of the qualities of the Yorkshire pig, an English breed, that I decided to try some. Louis claimed they require little care, rustle well in legume and grass pasture, and are bred up for bacon and ham production.

Shortly after his visit, I bought eight bred sows from C. E. Rhoad, Washington Court House, Ohio. A boar came from one of Mr. Rhoad's neighbors. The pigs did well, and later I bought ten more gilts from Mr. Rhoad. The Ohio boar did not suit me so I bought a better one from Burgess Farm, Waco, Texas.

Our breeding sows and boars are pastured and are given only a little corn. These hogs are very thrifty. The piggy sows are moved to a barn to farrow, where they remain until the young are a week old. The sows are fed hog mash that increases milk production and maintains vigor. Sows and pigs have done well, and we wean about ten young ones per sow. When a litter is a week old, sow and pigs are turned into a large, hog-tight, irrigated alfalfa pasture.

137

These hog traps are provided with shelter houses, hog feeders, water, and shade from large native oak, elm, or walnut trees.

The sows are generous milkers, and their litters show it. Yorkshire sows' mothering instincts are strongly developed. Several sows are pastured together, and young pigs nurse any of the sows, who seem to be perfectly willing to allow this trespass by the youngsters.

Hogs have proved to be a profitable venture, and I plan to continue and enlarge the business. All breeding hogs are registered. I get $20 each for gilts at weaning time, and gilts of breeding age are sold for $50 each. Most of the males go to market as barrows, but a few of the best are sold for breeding purposes. Boars of weaning age are sold for $25, and those six months of age bring $65 each.

F.F.A. and 4-H Club boys and girls buy a good many of my hogs for their projects. The hog business generally is increasing in our area, and will provide a much needed market for maize, hegari, and other grain sorghums that do well here, where corn growing is hazardous because of summer droughts.

My barrows have been topping the Fort Worth market. They prime out on pasture and threshed maize at a cost that yields a reasonable profit. We pay 2 cents per pound for maize. It costs me about 10 cents to produce one pound of live porker. As long as hog prices are around 16 or 17 cents per pound liveweight, we can make good money from our Yorkshires.

At present, we are breeding ten sows per month, and in a few months, we will be able to breed eight sows a week.

At this last rate, we can market a truck load of hogs each week. This plan will also provide as many registered breeding animals as can be readily sold at a reasonable profit.

I am getting a lot of pleasure watching my hog business develop. I have found out that hogs are only as dirty as their owners force them to be. We provide clean, roomy quarters, and under such conditions, hogs are naturally clean and do not live up to the tradition that brands them as symbols of filthiness.

Chapter 12

THE WILDLIFE ON FLAT TOP RANCH

William R. Van Dersal

Actually the full story of wildlife on this land is a long one, and one that is not too easy to reconstruct. Possibly the use of this area by man began in centuries past when the Indians periodically burned the prairies in pursuit of game. Later on, in the beginning of the nineteenth century, the gently rolling prairies resounded to the hoofbeats of wild horses escaped from white men and hunted both by them and by the Indians. But for our purposes, perhaps the story begins in earnest when the earliest settlers in Central Texas began using the land for farming and the game for food and sport.

In the middle of the last century, several pioneer families took up land in and around the forks of the Bosque River and the bottom lands of the Brazos. According to the journals they kept, these people traveled and hunted over Flat Top land, their hogs ranged over it, and some of their cattle grazed its grasses. One of the earliest was Colonel Buck Barry, who came in about 1845, and who undertook, as soon as he could, to plow the land and plant it to corn, wheat, oats, potatoes, and other crops.

"One of the most diverting forms of recreation open to the frontier settler was hunting," wrote the Colonel in *A Texas Ranger and Frontiersman,* edited by James K. Greer

140

(Dallas, 1932). "I enjoyed hunting and did a lot of it both for the sport and the meat to be had.

"Game was plentiful, and of numerous kinds. We had bear, panthers, deer, otter, wolves, cats, some buffalo, antelope, turkeys, prairie chickens, ducks, geese, and birds too numerous to mention. We seldom wanted for game to eat during the several years population remained sparse.

"Deer and turkey were not difficult to kill, although they soon learned to make themselves hard to find. There were pelt animals in plenty, but we were not interested in trapping, although we poisoned wolves because they preyed on young stock.

"The other outstanding sport we enjoyed, but which we also made yield some substance, was fishing." On the North Bosque he "caught over one hundred [fish] by seining with wagon-sheets sewn together," and he adds, ". . . we caught plenty of good sized ones. Fish frys were held at intervals during the summer, and we always had one on the Fourth of July."

Near by, the Colonel's neighbor, called Ken Cary by author James K. Greer in his book, *Bois D'Arc to Barbed Wire* (Dallas, 1936), but probably the author's own father, settled a few years later within sight of Flat Top Mountain. Cary recites the same list of wild game and adds to it coyotes, foxes, squirrels, raccoons, and jackrabbits. He also notes the presence of bobwhites, meadowlarks, mockingbirds, crows, and herons. By the end of the Civil War, he says, the antelope were beginning to disappear, and during the 1870's, they became very scarce, and finally were gone altogether.

141

During the last half of the century, more settlers came
in to take up land, and the hunting pressure on wild game
increased as the population grew. Commercial hunters—
Indians and whites alike—operated in this area, and they
sent a steady stream of hides and meat to Fort Worth and
Waco for shipment to eastern markets. Deer, buffalo, and
antelope, as long as they lasted, were prominent in this
trade, but even quail and prairie chickens were still being
killed and shipped in quantity lots as late as 1892.

Dates by which the various species disappeared from the
Flat Top area are uncertain, and the records of their passing
are meager. But such vast changes in the native habitat
of prairie wildlife were taking place that many species could
not possibly have survived even if the commercial hunters
had left them alone. As the grasslands were plowed and
cultivated and the rich covering of grasses entirely eliminated, the mammals and birds dependent on grass would
have been crowded into the remnants. As the rest of the
grassland was fenced and subjected to constantly heavier
grazing, trees and brush began to invade the prairies. Cedar
and oak scrub, so physically dense as almost to prohibit the
passage of larger animals, began to choke the grassland,
as has already been noted in an earlier chapter. Where the
brush did not come in, the cover became unbelievably poor,
thin, and weedy. On sizable areas, the lush prairie grasses
disappeared almost entirely. The bare soil showed through
the annual grasses and weeds, many of them not native
even to the Western Hemisphere, let alone to Texas. Great
piles of flatbladed opuntia cactus began to appear, then

became common. Livestock enterprises came—and are still coming—to a miserable conclusion. So did many farms. Gullies dissected the landscape; stream beds changed to ravines that carried flash floods after heavy rains, and became dry and dusty afterwards. Springs dried up.

Under such monstrously unwise use of these lovely prairie lands, it is little wonder that many of the associated wild creatures disappeared. All species of wildlife must have their preferred habitats in which to live. With changes in those habitats come changes in the kind and abundance of the birds and mammals. Historically, almost everywhere in North America, the larger animals were the first to go. In 1845, the German geologist and naturalist, Ferdinand Roemer, counted four hundred buffalo twenty miles from Flat Top, and wrote of the prairies crisscrossed in every direction with buffalo trails. But the buffalo has been gone from this area for some three-quarters of a century. The antelope, as Cary noted, was gone by 1880. The white-tailed deer lasted longer; in 1932, two bucks were killed in Bosque County, and the fact was sufficiently unusual to merit attention in the Meridian newspapers.

By the time Pettit acquired Flat Top Ranch, nearly all the larger animals were gone. Besides the ones already mentioned, the bears were gone, as were the panthers. So also were the turkeys, the prairie chickens, and the beaver. Waterfowl flew over going south or returning north; there was almost no place to stop on Flat Top because there was no water. And because there was no water, and because the flowing streams had been cut to storm sewers for flash

143

floods, there were no fish. No fish for mink, no fish for otter, for herons, for cranes, or for other species that must live on fish and other water creatures.

To the best of his knowledge, the owner thinks there were about six coveys of quail on Flat Top in 1938–39, and from a survey of near-by worn-out lands, it is hard to believe there could have been any at all. There were a few wolves, and there were some coyotes and wildcats. Rattlesnakes were there still, and buzzards. And there were many small birds and mammals.

There exists no documented history of Flat Top wildlife. No one, not even Colonel Barry, made lists of all the birds and mammals, and no game counts were made in the beginning nor during the one hundred years of exploitation. It is possible now to deduce these things largely from such sources as (1) the near-by lands and their wildlife inhabitants, (2) the recorded observations of early settlers or travelers, (3) the known relationship between the prairie vegetation and the wildlife it will support, and (4) the observations made on Flat Top by its owner, members of his staff, and visiting biologists.

These comparisons and relationships cannot be precise, and the conclusions derived from them can scarcely be considered the result of a scientific study. The situation is further complicated by many other factors. We can only surmise that probably there was at one time an increase in the rodents that feed on weeds in proportion to the decrease in grass and the increase in those weeds. If so, there would have been an increase, too, in the hawks and owls, coyotes, and snakes that feed upon the rodents. Jackrabbits must have increased as well; certainly these animals are very commonly associated with overgrazed ranges, although they were by no means absent on the virgin lands, as Ken Cary notes. The introduction of barbwire fences would have hampered the ranging of certain of the animals, notably antelope. The replenishment of habitats once destroyed and now recreated has not been, and possibly could not have been, made by introduction of precisely the same sub-species of birds or mammals as originally occurred there. Even the present-day, relatively lush habitats have not yet reached their fullest expression—marred at the moment by the sixth year of the worst drought in historical times. Many other uncertainties could be listed.

At any rate, the story of wildlife on Flat Top is a long one, and a complicated one. And it is a story as yet without an end. But in 1956, as this was written, this is where it had come:

Today there is a herd of white-tailed deer on Flat Top Ranch estimated at between 500 and 1,000 animals, depending on the time of year. In 1955, a survey by the Texas Game, Fish, and Oyster Commission put the number at about 1,000. In 1956, in September, the author counted 244 deer on some two hundred acres of recently cut alfalfa in one evening. The following evening there were 210 on the same fields. The animals certainly tallied were estimated to be about two-thirds of those present but difficult to see or uncertainly tallied—for a total of some 300. On the remainder of the ranch, on the same evenings, individuals or groups of two to four were observed frequently enough to justify a conservative estimate of one deer per

145

50 acres—for a total of more than 300. This amounts to at least 600 deer that must have been on the ranch at that particular time.

This herd has resulted from 49 animals released on the ranch in 1946 by the Texas Game Commission, plus 151 animals released on neighboring ranches from 1946 to 1948. The deer released, Pettit says, were "quite small," and were trapped on the King Ranch. After a few years, the deer that were seen were distinctly larger—one buck taken in 1955 weighing 170 pounds dressed, which is a big animal as whitetails go. This increase in size has not only been noted in white-tailed deer, but also in quail, and in Hereford cattle brought into the ranch from southern Texas. This size increase in deer has been noted before by biologists in many places, and it is apparently associated with better soils and the consequently better forage. In general, the studies show that deer enjoying a plentiful, varied, and nutritious food supply weigh much more than those where food is less plentiful (i.e., or where the deer are more crowded, which amounts to the same thing).

It is unusual to drive a few miles on any part of the road system on the ranch without seeing a few deer, especially in the early morning or evening. Their white tails flash most commonly along the edges of the woods near the streams or on the rougher, higher elevations. The animals are more abundant in late fall and winter; they come in to feed on hay put out for livestock and on the alfalfa fields. Pettit says he has observed deer five to ten miles away headed toward Flat Top in the evening, and has seen them leaving in the early morning.

146

The value put on these deer is about $50 a head, based on actual hunting sales, discussed later. At this rate, there is a herd worth $25,000 to $50,000 on this ranch.

In 1945, there was a herd of eighty antelope on the ranch, resulting from the release of ten does and six bucks in 1941 by the Texas Game Commission. This rapid increase speaks well for the conditions on the ranch, but the herd shortly went to pieces for other reasons. Twenty-five does escaped through a water gap and could not be recovered. The remaining animals then consisted of two-thirds bucks and one-third does. The bucks fought among themselves, and many died from infections of their wounds. The victor among the males was so successful in keeping the does herded into one corner of the pasture that they were soon starving.

The animals repeatedly refused feed offered them, such as alfalfa hay, or even green alfalfa. Thus the herd apparently could not be fed. Some fences were taken down to permit the survivors to get into other pastures, and they got along satisfactorily until 1951 when, because of severe drought, there were very few green weeds. By 1953 only three does were left.

That year two bucks were brought in, and the herd began to increase again; in 1956 it had grown to fifteen animals. Plans now are to build small gaps in the fences on Flat Top and on adjoining ranches. Rough Creek Ranch, on the north, owned by Major W. F. Long and his wife, Pettit's son-in-law and daughter, now has a herd of eighteen antelope. The two ranches together will offer an area of 29,000 acres, which should be enough for a herd of as many as

147

three hundred to five hundred animals, providing conditions are fully suitable for them. Under original conditions, a territory this size is believed to have carried as many as one thousand animals.

The antelope on both Flat Top and Rough Creek were in fairly good condition as observed in September, 1956. They could have been fatter, and they were possibly tamer than they should be. Antelope will feed upon the prairie grasses —both green grass and dry grass, as proved by stomach contents examined in many specimens. They will eat the seed heads and buds of many "weeds." Possibly as the alfalfa fields of Flat Top are made available to the herd, there may be some improvement in it.

As to the area these animals must have in order to thrive, there is conflicting opinion. Antelope have been successfully kept on ranches no larger than Flat Top, and there are many records of these animals staying within two to six miles of one spot the year round. Yet the migratory habits of these animals are also well known, and in some areas the animals do travel long distances. The migrations are generally local and irregular. At any rate, given the extensive territory that will be opened up by the fence gaps in the two ranches, conditions may be improved for these interesting animals.

There are believed to be about a thousand turkeys on and around Flat Top Ranch, the result of releasing a small flock in 1945. A few years before that, in 1941, twenty-four birds from south Texas were turned loose on the open range after several months of confinement. They were not successful. The later release, of birds obtained from the Clear Fork of the Brazos River, was the one that multiplied so well.

These birds range widely, and one banded bird from Flat Top was captured near Fort Worth, seventy-five miles away. Even so, during the winter, when food becomes scarce elsewhere, a great many of the birds return to the ranch. As with many other kinds of wildlife on this ranch, the automatic feeders full of corn, oats, and linseed cake are what bring them home or keep them there.

No turkeys may be shot on Flat Top. Pettit feels that the great quantities of grasshoppers these birds eat more than pays for their keep. Actually, since their numbers on the ranch are lowest during the height of the grasshopper season, and since grasshoppers are also devoured by road-runners, scissor-tailed flycatchers, skunks, and many other forms of wildlife on the ranch, it would not affect the grass-hopper population noticeably if the turkeys were subject to light hunting. Nor, in view of the success of these birds, would it be likely to damage the flock.

Bobwhite quail are plentiful on the ranch. On almost any day during the fall, a number of coveys can be flushed on a short trip over the ranch roads. In the spring, the clear whistling of the males can be heard anywhere on the place. The birds frequent the areas in and about the wooded creek beds, but they range far afield in the luxuriant grasses of the pastures.

Quail hunting is available on the ranch for a fee, with a guaranteed limit of birds. Trained dogs are available, and when the hunter has had his sport, and if by chance he is

149

short of the bag limit, the difference is made up to him in dressed birds from the quail farm. Flat Top raises about ten thousand quail a year, and sells fertile eggs, dressed birds, or live birds for release. The enterprise pays for itself, and in addition, birds are released at the quail pens periodically. Gradually they range away from the pens, out into the coverts on the ranch. They get wild quickly, Pettit says, and even with dogs, hunters can seldom get more than ten or twelve birds out of twenty-five immediately after release.

Some five hundred birds were released to start with, when the grass and other cover was judged to be suitable. From these, plus the releases made from the quail pens, the present abundance has resulted. "No way to wake up in the morning as nice as to hear bobwhite quail talkin'," says the owner of Flat Top.

Scaled quail, often called blue quail, were also released on the place, but have not succeeded in establishing themselves. Of the 125 birds released originally, a few were seen from time to time for several years, but they seem by now to have disappeared completely.

Despite the fact that prairie chickens were hunted in this area by early settlers and were reported as apparently quite abundant, two attempts to re-establish them have proved relatively unsuccessful. A trial was made in 1951, and again in 1953, with the help of the Texas Game Commission. In both trials, the birds were observed once or twice a few weeks afterwards, but then they disappeared. In December of 1956, however, four prairie chickens were discovered, probably from the 1953 planting.

No one knows with certainty why the trials failed. The number released could have been too few. The manner of their release might not have been the best way to do it, although great pains were taken to do the job as carefully as possible. There is the possibility that the fuller recovery of the grassland may ensure successful re-establishment of these prairie birds later on. At any rate, the trial will be made. It would be a wonderful thing to have prairie chickens on this ranch, both because of their hunting possibilities and because they are an integral part of the locale. One expects to see them, almost as a matter of course, on prairie land in as good condition as on this ranch.

Mourning doves are abundant on Flat Top the year round, except for a short period when cool weather begins. These birds are migratory, of course, and those present in the summer fly south when the weather cools in the fall. Birds from the north soon come in to replace them, and the reverse process takes place in the spring—the birds that wintered to the southward come back to nest on the ranch.

During the open season, there is excellent dove hunting on the ranch. The birds become wild and tricky, and it takes a good shot to bring one down. The birds are fine eating, and well worth the trouble. In a single day, one can see hundreds in traveling over the roads of the ranch.

In early September of each year, the ducks begin to arrive on the ranch. With the appearance of the first ones, feed is put out on the shore of House Lake—the one close to the ranch house. Each year about $500 worth of corn is used, always on the one lake, where no birds are ever hunted. There is a great flight in to the lake each evening when the

151

feed is scattered. Pettit says this operation is not at all profitable, except in the interest he has in watching the birds. From about mid-November through the season, as much as fifty pounds of corn per day is distributed in this fashion.

Teal are usually first to come in the fall and last to leave in the spring. Pintails come in soon after, then mallards, canvasbacks, and many others. All these species are wintering at Flat Top. None of them has been known to raise young there. A pair of Canadian geese with clipped wings, secured from the Texas Game Commission, have been on the lakes for over a year, but whether they will breed or not remains to be seen.

Pettit estimates the number of ducks on the ranch during the winter at three thousand to five thousand. He says as he has continued the feeding program more birds have come in each year. The birds are not heavily hunted, and relatively few are shot. The owner says that not more than one hundred birds are taken in any one year. There is, in the forty-three lakes on the ranch, and in the streams and sloughs, a vast area suitable for waterfowl, and it is abundantly used.

There are about 450 to 500 surface acres of water on this ranch when the reservoirs are full. If they were stocked to capacity and managed without fertilization, they might produce up to 200 pounds of fish per acre per year. This would total 90,000 to 100,000 pounds—45 to 50 tons. If the waters were fertilized, the yield could probably be doubled, or very nearly so. Hence, on this ranch, in normal seasons, it might be possible to produce between 90 and 100 tons of fish per year—if anyone wanted that much! The value of

Only twelve pigs show here, but this Yorkshire sow had seventeen in this litter.

A good feed trough made of steel barrels cut in half and welded together.

A permanent feed trough of rock and concrete.

the fishing—strictly in terms of cash, to say nothing of the sport—would be about $36,000 per year on unfertilized waters and nearer $75,000 if the lakes were fertilized—pricing the fish at an average of 40 cents a pound.

However, fishing in the waters of the ranch is pretty largely limited to members of the ranch family and friends of the owner. Because the waters are fished relatively lightly, the annual production is far below what it might be if the owner desired to manage the waters and produce an annual crop. The light fishing pressure commonly results, however, in fine large fish, especially largemouth bass. The overstocking is intended by the owner to result in hungry fish, working their way up and down the river as the ponds overflow. He believes this should help provide fishing for many people both upstream and down as far as the Brazos.

"One of the reasons why there have been no labor troubles on this ranch," says the owner, "is because the only thing a woman has to do here to have excellent fish for dinner is to want to!" And it is true that a fine string of good fish is almost guaranteed to the fisherman who will spend an hour or two casting, or trolling, or bait-fishing in the waters over the area. As an example, one man with an artificial bait caught thirty fish totaling one hundred pounds in an hour and a half.

As each water-impoundment has been completed, it has been variously stocked with bluegills, redears, crappies, channel cats, and bass. These fish provide an abundance for the people who live on the ranch, and the meat is a saving of some size on the grocery bills.

Besides the game birds and mammals, the seventeen

thousand acres of this ranch support a tremendous population of other wildlife in remarkable abundance and great variety.

Conspicuous because of their beauty and spirit are the scissor-tailed flycatchers. These birds seem to be everywhere in the open land, and their graceful flight, long tails, and flashing color is something to attract constant attention. In September of 1956, twenty-six of these birds were observed in driving over a 4,300-foot strip of grass used for an airplane landing field.

There are beaver in the streams, although they build no dams. Originally five animals were released on the adjoining ranch, and Pettit estimates that twenty-five to fifty are on Flat Top now (which has more water than does the adjoining ranch). These beaver are bank-dwellers, and their workings can be seen from time to time where they have cut trees. The value to the ranch would be considerable if the animals would build dams and back up water to raise the stream levels (and associated adjacent water tables). However, there are no aspens on the ranch and relatively few willows. Generally, beaver do best where these trees are abundant. There is a remote possibility that the transplanted beaver were not dam-builders, but bank-dwellers, and that dams might be built if animals were trapped in areas where dam-building is customary. The weight of evidence seems to be against this possibility, but it should be tried. After all, some beaver do build dams out of apple trees or cornstalks, and the aspen and willow may not be as essential as some wildlife specialists believe.

Raccoons, skunks, and armadillos are quite common. Almost any evening, a tour of the ranch will enable an observer to see these animals a number of times in a few miles. Everywhere one drives, there are jackrabbits, and on a night drive, these long-eared creatures seem always to be bounding along in the glare of the headlights. There are marsh rabbits, cottontail rabbits, ring-tailed cats, minks, opossums, and red and gray foxes on the ranch. Squirrels are common enough, particularly in the years when the acorn crop is abundant. Very rarely, there are occasional wolves, coyotes, or bobcats.

About the lakes, there are many kinds of water and shorebirds, that come and go with the seasons. Herons, killdeer, and a host of others can be seen nearly any time, and turtles and bullfrogs of some size. Road runners there are, with ruffled feathers and crazy antics. There are a few golden eagles, many kinds of hawks and owls. And there are cardinals, mockingbirds, bluebirds, meadowlarks, blackbirds, cowbirds, swallows, and a host of others, which, if listed, would include most, if not all, of the native and migratory birds to be found in Central Texas. All are interesting wild species, and all are contributing to making Flat Top a more interesting place in which to live.

There are a number of wild creatures that were once on the ranch or that are still present that are not wanted. Some of them are gone, and would not be permitted to remain should they turn up again. Bears are in this group, and so are panthers. Buffalo are included, too, because the bulls are extremely hard to hold within fenced areas, and a

155

project involving registered Hereford cattle of high value can scarcely be permitted to include the American bison, regardless of how interesting this animal may be.

Some of the undesirable wildlife species may appear from time to time, and when they do, they are shot on sight or hunted down and killed. Rattlesnakes are in this group, as well as copperheads. The danger to the people on the ranch and to the livestock from these poisonous snakes is too great to risk. There is a standing rule on the ranch that rattlers are to be killed when seen, ahead of anything else that may be going on. There is a bounty paid of 50 cents per "rattle," and about thirty-five to fifty of the payments are collected each year. The owner suspects that boys bring in the rattles from snakes killed on neighboring ranches as well as on Flat Top, but he pays without question. Conversely, however, orders are to leave all sharp-tailed snakes alone.

Wolves are in this same group, and have been trapped out; the destruction of these animals was first undertaken, as already noted, by Colonel Barry, more than one hundred years ago. Coyotes are rare on the place, but would be shot if seen. Bobcats, for which there is a ranch bounty of $10.00, are on the list, and two to four are killed each winter. Red and gray foxes are also on the list, with a bounty of $5.00 for each one trapped. Usually about ten to fifteen are caught each year.

In the belief that domestic cats gone wild are serious enemies of quail, Flat Top policy is to shoot any cat more than 150 yards away from any house on the ranch. Pettit believes that any farmer wanting to be successful with quail should get rid of his house cats first. And while there is doubt about this, feral cats are very rare on the ranch.

With the exception of Cooper and sharp-tailed hawks, the hawks are let alone. The "blue darters" are recognized as predatory on young poultry as well as game birds, and they are shot when seen. The great soaring hawks are believed to pay for themselves in rodents and rabbits killed. Owls, too, are let alone, for their value in rodent destruction.

Lastly, there is a group of nuisance animals that are unprotected on this ranch. They may be killed if desired (within legal limits, of course, if there are such). Included here are skunks, because of their foul odor, jackrabbits, crows, and armadillos caught digging up flower beds about the houses, and raccoons, when they get too numerous. Coons have a habit of selecting and scattering the linseed pellets from the creep feeders put out for the calves. Occasionally, they are cut down in numbers because of this habit.

Buzzards would be on this list as well, if they were not protected. They clean up carrion to be sure, but they go from dead animals to the watering troughs for water and Pettit feels that they can spread disease. After all, when a $10,000 bull drinks from such a trough, no one likes to take the chance of having dead and possibly diseased animal matter floating before the Hereford's nose.

"Whatever I do on the ranch, I would like for there to be a little profit in it," says Charles Pettit, and on this basis he sells hunting privileges. Each year some 150 hunters pay $25 a day for the privilege of hunting on the ranch. About half of them get a deer, so that the ranch realizes about $50 for each deer killed.

157

In addition, an area of 1,000 acres with particularly choice hunting is leased for $2,500 a year to a group of businessmen. This land is also used for the production of cattle as well as hogs. There is included a clubhouse for the benefit of the group.

Possibly $10,000 a year is realized on the ranch from the sale of hunting and fishing privileges. The value of fishing and hunting to the residents of the ranch is hard to estimate, but is obviously considerable. But there are other values. "Nothing has brought me into association with a bunch of good fellows, and brought the good out of *them*, any more than game," declares Flat Top's owner. And he goes on to speak with a smile of a group of his friends soon to gather at the ranch for a little hunting and some good fun generally. What price hunting rights?

Actually the hunting—and the fishing—pressure on the wildlife of this ranch is very light. No turkeys are killed, twice as many quail are released as shot, possibly a hundred ducks are taken out of several thousand that gather there; seventy-five deer or so out of perhaps a thousand, no antelope of course, and the fishing of his friends and staff. Possibly, of all the wildlife on the ranch, doves come in for the heaviest hunting, but even these are not pursued beyond reasonably light bounds. "We raise lots more of everything than we destroy," says the owner, and his statement is clearly true.

"The more a man learns about this game business," he goes on to say, "the less he wants to kill the wild animals. I've pretty near quit. I can have more fun watching a beaver for two hours than most people get in twice that time.

Flat Top Wildlife

I find I'm nearly as much interested in these scissortails and beavers and road runners as I am in deer or turkeys or quail." And Flat Top itself is the expression of Charles Pettit's philosophy.

What total value accrues to the ranch enterprise from the many thousands of wild creatures living on the area would be difficult to estimate. The weed seed-destroying and insect-eating birds and mammals contribute a great deal, without question. So do the rodent-eating hawks, owls, and snakes. Such wildlife values as these are large in the aggregate. When they are added to the hunting pro-vided by the game, the sport and food from fish, and the pleasure to the ranch family of seeing and living among the many varied and interesting wild inhabitants, Charles Pettit thinks a little extra care is indeed well worth the cost.

The story of Flat Top Ranch is essentially a story of abused and mismanaged grassland that has been vastly im-proved. Plowed land unsuited for crops generally has been planted to native prairie grasses. The choking brush that invaded the destructively overgrazed prairies has been re-moved to make way for these same nutritious plants. The dried-up springs and streams are flowing again, even in drought years. And with the change from original prairie to destruction and back again, most of the associated wildlife has, in general, changed and returned or been returned along with the original vegetation.

But there should be no mistake about the "biological bal-ance" involved. The intent on Flat Top was not to return to the primeval conditions exemplified by the phrase, "bal-ance of nature," but to develop a balance of practical use to

159

man. Possibly other men would have developed a different kind of balance, although it is difficult to see how a better one could be achieved.

There are no buffalo to graze the prairie grasses now; their place was taken first by wild horses, then Longhorns, and now by Hereford cattle. There are many other changes from the original "balance of nature," if indeed there ever was such a thing under the dynamic and changing conditions that affect virgin land no less than everyday agriculture. Antelope cannot jump fences that keep cattle within bounds, even though deer can. Alfalfa from southwestern Asia was not in the schemes of vegetation original to this area, although its abundant presence possibly enables deer and other wild creatures to increase beyond the numbers once depending on the wild legumes, grass, and browse. There are many things for wildlife to eat among the introduced weeds that were absent a hundred years ago, to say nothing of the abundant and choice food available in the creep feeders set out for Hereford calves. There is a drain on certain snakes and skunks and crows and such, and an enforced absence of the larger predators—the bears, wolves, panthers, bobcats, and coyotes.

There is a vast extent of land involved in 17,000 acres, but not necessarily to antelope or turkey or prairie chickens, or even deer, accustomed to range quite as widely as they like. For lack of food and cover in surrounding country, Flat Top unquestionably harbors visiting animals, big and little, from season to season. There is considerably more water in total, and more water surface, on this piece of land than there was originally.

160

All these changes and many others, known as well as un-realized, complicate the story of wildlife here and make it difficult to piece together. They indicate, too, with reasonable certainty, that the original "balance of nature" can scarcely be restored. The fact is, *no one really wants it back.*

Nevertheless, a running balance can be struck, one that is practical in its use and value to man, and one in which those species of birds and mammals that are desired can live at home in the habitats that are at once in good balance with the soils that support them and with the domestic animals that use them. Such a practical balance has been tentatively reached on this ranch. It will be changed—it is *being* changed—with drought, and with the wet years that one day may follow. It will be changed as men's ideas change—about game limits, hunting seasons, predators, and interests of many kinds. But the first trial balance has been struck, in which most of the interesting animals of the original prairie grassland are now back on restored prairie grassland closely similar to what it was, but possibly just a little better in its water, food, and cover relationships for prairie wildlife.

The story of wildlife on Flat Top is necessarily a story without an end. A multitude of projects are designed to improve and make better a ranch already remarkable for its well-nigh unique progress. And included in these improvements are changes that may well affect the practical, but necessarily moving, balance between the land and the wildlife that lives upon it in association with man's own creatures.

Chapter 13

IMPROVEMENTS THAT WILL STAY
Martine Emert

PERMANENCE IS THE keynote of the Flat Top management. The man with the vision of a permanent ranch knows that the improvements on that ranch will reach maximum efficiency and economy only when they also are planned and built to stay.

The difference between starvation and prosperity is management. If the rancher is going to make money, he has to figure every item of expense very closely, including his own time and that of his employees (if any), and the cost of operating his motor vehicles. That is why the careful planning of the interrelationship of barns, fences, roads, water supplies, feed troughs, bridges, gates, and other improvements is a matter of so much importance. It costs at least ten cents a mile to operate a car or truck; therefore, unnecessary driving is a luxury the average rancher cannot afford. Good farm labor is often difficult to obtain, as any rancher knows, and the substitution of mechanization for labor can be a tremendous economy.

Starting from scratch requires long-range planning, and the gradual working out of that plan as money and labor become available. Here the rancher is faced with the problem of doing the essential things first. A very important first move for the average rancher would be to become a co-

162

operator in his local soil conservation district. From these trained technicians, assigned to the district by the Soil Conservation Service, he can get a great deal of very valuable help without cost; the district frequently owns and rents to its members pieces of machinery that the rancher might not feel able to buy; and from the district he can get a soil inventory or range site map on an aerial photograph of his place. The Flat Top Ranch has long been a co-operator with the Bosque Soil Conservation District.

With the aid of the aerial photograph and the technicians, the farmer or rancher will find his job of planning is simplified. The location of his house in relation to barns, water supplies, and roads is important. A pure water supply that cannot possibly be contaminated from any seepage from the barns, and a location far enough away from any barn where animals are to be kept to prevent odors and flies in the house, are other important considerations.

Any ranch or stock farm needs at least two barns—one for hay, and the other for grain and feed. Both should include facilities to take care of livestock.

A barn is more than just a building. To be economical, it must be useful, convenient, and a permanent and handsome addition to the ranch. Barns serve many purposes. In some parts of the United States, a barn is essential for keeping the livestock warm during the cold winter months, but in most of Texas, it is much more important for keeping cattle cool during the heat of the summer. A barn is also used for grinding, mixing, and storing feed, and for keeping quantities of hay. It is a convenient place for calving, for weaning the young, or for caring for the sick or injured animals.

163

Young cattle are trained to be handled in a barn, and to the barn come purchasers to buy the animals gathered there for sale. Seed, salt, supplements, spray materials, machinery, and other necessary equipment may be stored there—and any rancher can think of a dozen more uses to which he puts this very essential building. But regardless of the purpose for which the barn is built, its location should be chosen with care, and its construction should be permanent.

In locating the feed barn, take into consideration the way in which the ranch is divided into pastures and fields, where the water and feed troughs are to be placed, and where the roads and fences will be. Because of that ten-cents-a-mile cost of hauling, a feed barn should be located where it is possible to get the feed from the field to the barn for storage, and from the barn to the pastures and feed troughs with the least possible transportation. And, of course, the barn has to have a water supply and be on accessible roads.

With the location decided upon, construction follows. A wooden barn is cheaper to build, but it is a fire hazard. Even with costly painting every few years or so, the wood deteriorates. Too often the sides sag, the doors drag and eventually break down, the wood rots, the boards fall out, and the barn becomes a useless eyesore or falls victim to fire or wind. Then a new one has to be built. You have seen that happen to hundreds of barns.

If a wooden barn costs $1,000 to build and lasts ten years, it has cost the rancher $100 a year. A galvanized iron or rock or concrete barn of similar size may cost $2,500 to build, but can be so well constructed that it will last at least one hundred years, thereby costing less than $25 a year. Furthermore, the wooden barn requires constant costly maintenance, often running into several hundreds of dollars during the lifetime of the barn, while the more permanent barns require very little maintenance. In the long run the permanent barn is by far the cheapest. In addition, it has the great advantage of being fireproof, virtually tornado proof, and, because it will last so long, its entire cost can eventually be depreciated from your income tax.

Rock has been the main structural material used on the Flat Top Ranch, because there is so much of it there. For some of the structures, the rock was set in place by a local stone mason. The oldest and largest barn was economically built by setting up forms and pouring in rock and concrete. Anyone can do this, as no expensive skilled labor is required. Either one of these will blend into the landscape and last just about forever. If rock is not available, either concrete or corrugated iron will do an equally good job, require little maintenance, and always look like new.

With a view to maximum economy in labor, this feed barn was built on two levels against a little hill, with roads serving both levels. Feed is unloaded from above so that it can be dumped from the trucks into the storage bins by gravity, instead of having to be lifted. Any man with or without an aching back can appreciate this muscle-saving arrangement. Since the upper level need not be more than ten feet above the lower, there will be few ranchers who cannot find a convenient hill that will permit them to take advantage of this saving. Of course, all loading of feed taken from storage will be from below, with the floor of the barn on a level with the bed of a truck, so that, again, no lifting is required.

165

This feed barn is in the form of an "L," with a mill for grinding, mixing, and sacking feed in the center of one side, flanked by corn cribs on one end and storage bins for oats on the other. A distinctive feature of this mill is its system of conveyors, both overhead and in the floor, to perform all the labor of moving feed stuffs from bins and cribs to grinders, scales, and mixers. Screw or belt type conveyors in the barn may sound like an extravagance, but their utility is very much the same as electricity in the house. These conveyors will more than pay for themselves within a few years in the dollars and cents value of the time and labor saved, and any rancher would do well to investigate their cost and utility in relation to the cost of labor as he plans a feed barn.

In keeping with the idea that it is advisable to have a place to care for animals in connection with the feed barn, the lower story of the second side of the "L" has many stalls for cattle. On the Flat Top Ranch, all stalls are open to the south and walled on the north, so that the animals will be protected from the icy "northers" that occasionally sweep the prairies. These stalls are equipped with feed and drinking troughs made of concrete for permanence and complete sanitation. At one end, there is a small veterinary laboratory with all the common medicines, as well as a sink, refrigerator, and other equipment for the care of ailing or injured animals.

On the upper level of this section, trucks can be driven into the building from the upper road. This makes it possible to unload out of the rain or other bad weather conditions, or to leave loaded trucks parked overnight. Because of the weight of the trucks, it was necessary to support this floor with a couple of steel I-beams. The rancher who does not wish to go to this expense can make his second-story loading dock on a level with the truck bed to avoid any lifting, and not drive the trucks inside. At Flat Top, this floor is used for the storage of feed, grass seed, spray materials, and countless other items.

In connection with a feed barn, corrals and traps for the handling of the animals and a convenient loading chute are usually needed. A large outfit will find a set of scales for weighing trucks and cattle, and a dipping vat, very useful.

At Flat Top the concrete vat is built with a curbed concrete platform where the animals can remain until they stop dripping. This platform slopes slightly toward the vat, and the expensive dip runs back into the vat to be used over again, thereby reducing dipping costs. The cattle are dipped once or twice a year, as there is no other way of getting rid of lice and ticks. It is interesting to see how much more contented the cattle are afterwards, as though they really felt good.

The other essential barn is the hay barn, which should be a separate structure because of the danger of fire in hay. An aerial photograph (or a detailed map of the ranch) will be helpful in choosing the location for this building. Even small operators may find it more economical and convenient to have several small hay barns strategically located rather than one large barn. In that way, if lightning strikes or a grass fire gets started, only a part (but not all) of the hay will be destroyed.

Flat Top uses both rock and corrugated iron hay barns, but the structural features are essentially the same. First,

167

provision for maximum convenience in loading and unload-
ing, and second, provision for abundant air circulation to
prevent the hay from heating.

There is a little rock barn on the Flat Top that has proved
to be mighty useful, and might serve as a model for the
rancher who only plans one such barn. This was originally
built as a general utility barn, and can be turned to many
uses. At various times, it has served as a sales barn, and as
a place to feed cattle, but now it is being used primarily
as a hay barn. Each rancher will determine his own dimensions according to his needs and the lay of the land, but the
same principles apply. Doors on the east and west ends
should be large enough to drive a loaded truck right through
the building. Posts supporting the roof form a center aisle,
with ample space for hay on both sides. The Flat Top hay
barns are one hundred feet long by forty feet wide, and the
aisle posts are twenty-two feet high, supporting a corrugated iron roof made in broken gable design to give maximum storage capacity. Two hundred tons of hay may be
stored in a building with these dimensions without obstruct-
ing the center aisle. If desired, another one hundred tons
may be placed in the center by backing the trucks in from
each end.

Across the north wall, there is a row of windows for ventilation, and the south side (similar to the feed barn) has
stalls, covered by a corrugated iron shed roof. These stalls
are open to the outside and also open to the hay barn. This
makes a complete ventilating system for the hay, as well
as a protected place to get thirty or forty head of cattle in
out of the weather, for weaning of calves, or for other pur-

This small but durable rock barn has a sturdy corral made of cement posts with the spaces between filled in solidly with cedar stays.

The antelope herd in 1957.

A permanent cattle guard constructed of pipe supported by I-beams resting on concrete.

This cement bridge has a large watergate in the middle to take care of the normal flow of East Bosque Creek. Floods can flow over the bridge without damaging it or the road approaches.

poses. At one end of the stalls, there is a small room in which feed in sacks is stored. Adjacent to the stalls are the necessary corrals, traps, and feed and water troughs for handling the animals. It is highly efficient, will not burn, will last indefinitely, requires little or no upkeep, and always looks like new. It can be built by anyone who has the rocks near by, and in the long run, the cost will be much less than a series of wooden barns.

There are four corrugated iron hay barns on the Flat Top Ranch using the same principles as the rock barn, except that they have no stalls for cattle, and the solid walls begin about six feet above the ground. The open space is built like a corn crib to give ample ventilation to the hay, and yet keep the cattle out. These are located with the same care given to all buildings with relation to pastures, hayfields, roads, fences, etc., and serve as auxiliary storage on a place requiring more than one hay barn.

One of the most practical units on the ranch consists of a small rock barn with adjacent shed, corral, loading chute, and traps that are cheap and easy to construct; it requires little paint or repair, and will last indefinitely. These little barns are used for breeding, calving, caring for sick animals, for a bull that is troublesome, or for any other reason for separating a few animals from the herd. All are so situated that cattle can be driven in easily from two or three adjoining pastures, and represent one of the many efforts made to keep the cattle tame.

The little corral is only fifty by fifty-six feet in size. Attached on the north side is a shed and a ten-by-twenty-foot barn. A ten-foot gate completes that side. The other three

169

sides of the corral are of unique construction which is very cheap and almost indestructible. The posts are of concrete. The holes are dug eight feet apart and five feet deep. Forms are set on the ground five feet high, and the concrete is poured, making a ten-foot post that is as solid as the ground. While pouring, a piece of tin is placed in the concrete about eighteen inches from the top to form a hole, through which lengths of iron pipe are thrust to form the cross bars. Second-hand pipe can be used, and should not cost more than ten cents a lineal foot. Between the posts, a trench is dug in which cedar stays are placed upright as close together as possible and fastened tightly to the pipe with smooth galvanized wire.

The south side of the shed opens directly into the corral. The east end is a continuation of the corral fence. The north side is of native rock and is continuous with the end of the barn. A galvanized iron roof covers both the shed and barn. The small barn, which is used primarily for feed storage, has rock walls, a concrete floor, and plastered interior walls. Because it is snugly protected on the north and west, the barn and shed can easily shelter thirty or forty animals in the event of a bad storm in winter.

A concrete circular drinking trough, eighteen inches deep, is set in the fence so that half of it serves the animals inside the corral and the other half serves those in the adjoining trap—one trough doing the work of two.

The loading chute is a standard type used all over the ranch. A ramp of earth two and one-half or three feet wide is built the necessary length (about ten feet) to extend it easily to the height of the bed of a cattle truck. Across the high end, a concrete slab is constructed. The sides and gates of the chute are made of the second-hand pipe. These chutes are economical to build and are permanent as well as efficient.

On the Flat Top Ranch, the cattle are pastured throughout the year, but occasional supplemental feeding is necessary, and this requires feed troughs which are located as carefully as all the other improvements.

Because they are so much cheaper, concrete troughs are used. A good heavy wooden trough, bolted together, will not last many years. For any rancher who stays in business more than five years, the wooden trough is an expensive luxury. Where rock is available, a concrete trough costs only about 50 per cent more than a wooden one—and it is there practically forever.

For convenience and economy, most of the troughs on the ranch have the same dimensions and are poured into the same form. The trough is always located on sloping ground with one end higher than the other, so rain water will drain out through a hole left for that purpose in the lower end. Iron pipe, set on iron posts, divides the trough lengthwise in the middle to prevent the cattle from fighting and from getting into it. With a one-hundred-foot trough, sixty to seventy-five heifers can be fed at one time, but not more than forty old cows.

The very permanence of the concrete troughs presents a problem. Cattle get in the habit of staying around the feeding place and soon overgraze the area. The advantage of movable wooden troughs is that they can be easily shifted from place to place. The concrete trough cannot be moved,

171

so the problem is met by building two, one on each side of the pasture, and using them alternately.

Out on the range, a feed trough should be located on the south side of a rolling hill or clump of trees. A cow does not like to come out on the high hills when it is cold and windy, but will feed contentedly in a warmer, protected place that is well drained. Muddy conditions around feed troughs are unpleasant both for cattle and for the man who has to place the feed.

Some movable feed troughs are used on the ranch. These are made of two old oil drums cut in half lengthwise and welded together. Heavy supports made of angle irons and some pipe at the bottom complete the trough, which is easily moved, lasts much longer than a wooden one, but is not so permanent as concrete.

Water is one of the most necessary factors in successful ranch management, and has been mentioned in connection with each improvement as it has been described. The story of how the rainfall has been made to soak into the soil and become ground water so essential to the maintenance of lakes, streams, and wells, is told in another chapter. Wells, however, form part of the improvements. The wells, each at least two hundred feet deep, are cased to the full depth, so there will never be any cave-in. It is cheaper to case in the first place and have a permanent well than to leave the bottom open and have to drill again when the old well caves in.

Galvanized, instead of black, pipe is used because it will not rust. When setting the pipe, holes are drilled from the bottom of the well to the top of the water, even though it is as much as 150 feet. Then gravel, too large to go through the holes, is put alongside the casing. A well like this will last indefinitely, and is unlikely ever to need any further attention.

At first, the water troughs were built large enough for thirty or more cattle, but this proved to be an unnecessary expense. That many animals never seemed to want to drink at any one time. Now the troughs are quite small, only big enough for three or four. These little troughs are more sanitary. They can be washed out frequently and easily with a very small amount of water, and this is important in a section of the country where water is such a precious commodity. Some of the troughs are circular, and others are rectangular—about ten feet long, by three feet or less wide, and about eighteen inches deep. They are made of concrete and are permanent. Water comes to them by gravity, from the tank of a centrally located well, and is fed into the trough through a float valve with a ball that insures water at the same level all the time. The ball is essential, for the cattle will try to eat a device of any other shape.

Year by year—a little at a time—the pattern of permanent improvements expands. Such capital investments are essential to the efficient and economical operation of the ranch, reducing production costs and increasing profits.

Chapter 14

FENCES, ROADS, AND CATTLE GUARDS

Frank Reeves

THE OWNER OF Flat Top Ranch has given major consideration to three ranch projects that some ranchers are inclined to accept as unavoidable nuisances that must be endured rather than planned. They are his pasture fences, pasture roads, and the cattle guards on these roads.

It is not unusual for some visiting rancher to ask Pettit, "How in the world can you afford to spend so much on pasture fences, road building, and cattle guards?" His invariable answer is, "I cannot afford to do otherwise."

The man asking the question usually is thinking of the cost these items involve, without taking time to evaluate the service they render. Pettit is ready to admit that they cost a sizable amount of money, but he refuses to call them an unnecessary expense. He insists they are an investment, and the money that goes into them will continue to pay handsome returns on their cost by increasing the efficiency of the entire ranch operations.

These three items were a segment of the original development plans that were put into effect soon after Pettit took possession of the property. His belief is that individually and collectively they have repaid their cost by saving man-power hours, and while doing so, they have contributed liberally to the over-all ranch efficiency.

174

Fences, Roads, and Cattle Guards

The ranch has one hundred pastures and traps, varying in size according to the physical characteristics of their surroundings and the purpose they are intended to serve. The fences around each pasture or trap were put there for the specific purpose of keeping any animal or group of animals inside the pasture and all other animals on the outside.

A lot of experimenting has been done about the kind of fence that should be constructed according to its intended use. This has included woven wire enclosures and the number of wires needed, the distance between the posts, and whether to use a stay or stays between the posts, how deep the post should be in the ground, and the bracing of all corner posts.

The management has determined that seven strands of wire, three on one side and four on the other side of the post, will keep animals where they are supposed to stay, and at the same time discourage young bulls from fighting through the fence. The wires are staggered in their arrangement on the side of the post.

This large assortment of pastures makes it possible to control the grazing on different portions of the property. Certain pastures can be set aside for summer or winter use.

When one of the ranch hands says that an animal or group of animals can be found in a certain pasture, there is little chance for a misunderstanding about its exact location. Each pasture has a name, and at every cattle guard there is a painted sign giving the names of the pastures on each side of that guard.

The ranch road system has about 150 miles of roads inside the boundaries of the ranch property. These roads are

175

graded, ditched, and graveled. Permanent bridges or concrete crossings are over all the streams of any appreciable
size. Any time any of the hands set out to go some place
on the ranch, they have the assurance that they can make
a round trip in a minimum amount of time and with a
maximum amount of comfort. Weather conditions do not
close these roads to travel. If a load of feed or a piece of
equipment needs to be transferred from one portion of the
ranch to some other location, it is a very simple matter.
Not only do the roads cut down on travel time, but they
reduce the wear and tear on the vehicles that travel them.

There are forty-five cattle guards on an equal number of
fence lines where cars, pickups, and trucks cross frequently. These cattle guards save many man-power hours each
year as against the time that would be lost if all drivers
had to stop and get out and open and close gates. There is
a saving of gasoline by eliminating these stops.

The following specifications have been worked out for
standard procedure. First, a pit is dug about four and one-
half feet wide and ten feet long. A heavy wall of reinforced
concrete is put into the pit. The wall is made about eight
inches thick, and comes up even with the top of the ground.
At each end of the concrete, a frame is built, and this is
made into a concrete wing. The fences are then built up
against these wings. Four five-inch I-beams are placed
across the pit. Across these I-beams and running the length
of the pit are placed two-inch pipes with about six-inch
centers to cover the full width of the pit. This kind of construction will support extremely heavy loads. A big advantage for this kind of cattle guard is that it is practically

indestructible and requires a minimum amount of upkeep.

The ranch roads, in connection with the cattle guards, contribute liberally to the quick inspection of the ranch herds, and make it possible to do a very thorough job of seeing the cattle in the different pastures in a minimum amount of time and with a limited amount of help.

Two cowboys, with their two horses loaded in a trailer pulled by a car or pickup, can leave headquarters and in a comparatively short time reach any of the pastures. Here, they can unload their horses, ride the pasture, return to the trailer, reload their horses, and be on their way to another pasture. With this setup, two men can see more cattle in a day than could ten or twelve cowboys stationed at different places about the ranch. This cuts down on the necessity for numerous riders or horses.

The cattle guards contribute their part in saving time for the riders with their horses in a trailer. Another advantage is that they eliminate the mixing of cattle when a gate is left open. It is a pretty safe bet that sooner or later a gate would not be closed and then cattle would mix.

During the winter, when it is necessary to put out feed to livestock in the pasture, the feed trucks can travel much faster because of the ranch roads and the cattle guards. Not having to open and close gates is also a timesaver with the feed trucks.

Concrete feed troughs are used extensively for pasture feeding. They are not damaged by sun, rain, or weather of any kind. Their weight minimizes the chances for their being knocked over. Each trough has a drain hole for rain water to get out.

177

FRANK REEVES

Regular ranch help that has the know-how is used for the building of the cattle guards, troughs, roads, and fences. This lowers their cost as against depending on contract work by outsiders.

Chapter 15

HITTING THE JACKPOT

Martine Emert

WHEN SEVEN BULLS gain 4,025 pounds in eight months on three acres of land, that is spectacular. These purebred Hereford bull calves averaged 525 pounds when put on the land, and were worth $400 apiece. Eight months later, they averaged 1,100 pounds, and were worth $1,000 each. That three acres produced an income of $4,200 in eight months, or $175 per acre per month, less the cost of planting and irrigating the oats and sudan.

It was figures like this which led Flat Top's owner to revise his ideas of land values. Like many ranchers, he believed that it was necessary to have at least ten acres to run a cow. Therefore, you could not make money on land that cost more than $25 an acre. That may be true on dry hillsides, but fertile bottom lands along the creeks where irrigation is possible—well, that is a different story.

At the time the land was purchased, that three-acre plot was an almost impassable jungle of big trees, vines, briars, and underbrush, directly in the way of an easy crossing from the house to the barn. While Mr. Pettit was trying to ride through it one day, he was nearly dragged off his horse when it became frightened by a big rattlesnake. He turned the horse loose while he killed the snake—and found him-

179

self standing on a gold mine, although its true value was not fully appreciated until several years later.

This bit of bottom land had deep, rich soil and lay just below the House Lake, from which it could be irrigated easily. To get it ready for use, and to get rid of the snakes, it was cleared by bulldozing and burning—practices which have since been discontinued—at a (1939) cost of about $15 an acre. It was first put into a garden with vegetables and berry bushes, but subsequently the garden was moved to a more practical location nearer the main ranch house. For several years, it was planted to various crops, such as vetch and rye, oats and Madrid, sudan, all of them irrigated.

Then cattle were let in, and it was noticed how remarkably healthy they were, and how fast they grew. Some of the best calves on the ranch have been grown out in this small trap. For more than six years now, it has had five to seven bulls on it for eleven months out of each twelve. Oats and Madrid sweetclover, rotated with sudan, is a common planting. When the oats are cut, the sudan is sowed and watered, and in only a few days the cattle are back again. These animals are given a little supplemental feed and a little dry roughage, but that is all.

It is very difficult to estimate the value of the feed taken from these three acres over the years since they have been cleared. Yields have been constant and very high, due to the high fertility of the land and the periodic irrigation. Based on production, this land is easily worth $500 per acre —yet more profit in proportion is being made from cattle on $500-per-acre land than on $25-per-acre land.

180

Hitting the Jackpot

The location of this little "jackpot" is such that it is passed by nearly everyone who calls at the house, barn, or office. Visitors are immediately attracted by the fine condition of the cattle framed in the lush grass or oats. The advertising value of this spot is worth, alone, more than the cost of clearing, and it is easy to sell animals seen—and grown out in such ideal conditions.

The realization of the productive value of little corners along the creeks where the soil was fertile and could be irrigated led to the clearing of many more such little "jackpots." It often costs ten times as much to clear these areas as the shallow soils of the uplands, but the profit from them is so much greater, it makes the cost relatively negligible in the long run.

A rich fifteen-acre bottom land along Rough Creek was covered with very thick stands of trees, underbrush, vines, and briars. The cover was so thick it was impossible to ride or walk through it—even almost impossible to crawl through it. It was bulldozed in 1939 at a cost of about $12 per acre. Very little grass was found on it, and nothing at all was planted. In fact, it was neglected until about 1953, when a series of small dams, costing less than $200 apiece, was built on Rough Creek. One of these dams is opposite the fifteen acres and another, farther down, backs up some water alongside the lower part.

During the time the land was unused, native grass seed from the land above had been blown or washed down on it so that a good stand was established. As the water level rose behind the dams, it was noticed that the water table

181

was rising on both sides of the creek. The grass roots reached down into the water, and now this area produces more natural grass than any other land on the ranch.

Although the years 1955 and 1956 were very dry, nearly three tons of hay per acre were cut on this plot each June, after which the grass was left to mature a seed crop in the fall. By the first of November, when the seed was combined, the big bluestem and Indiangrass were over a man's head. Cattle were then turned in and grazed until the first of April.

The seed from the 1955 crop was used for planting on the ranch, but the two hundred pounds per acre harvested could have been sold at $1 per pound. This would have meant an income of $200 per acre, plus $50 for three tons of hay, plus five months of grazing. Since the cost of clearing the entire tract was only $180, it is obvious that the return per year on one acre is almost twice the total cost of clearing the whole fifteen. Furthermore, it has such a wonderful turf that, if cattle were allowed to run on it during the growing season, it could take care of two cows per acre and remain in good condition. One of the biggest advantages of a native hay meadow like this is that there is no expense of plowing or planting or cultivating. Each year the total production cost is just that of cutting the hay and combining the seed. Without doubt, this is another little "jackpot" worth at least $500 per acre. It really pays to clear the bottom lands.

Not all of the Flat Top "jackpots" were timber and brush covered. There is one little spot, thirteen acres in size, in a triangle where Flag Branch joins East Bosque Creek, that was part of an old farm. This had been a cleared field, but, like the rest of the farm, it was cottoned out and finally abandoned. At the time of purchase the house had fallen in, and the little field was so low in organic matter, phosphorus, and nitrogen that it could only support a poor stand of Johnsongrass and a few scrubby trees and bushes. Little erosion had occurred, however, as the place was nearly level. It had good potentiality, but its productivity was very low.

Little was done with it before 1950, except to pasture cattle on the Johnsongrass. Then it was cleared by plowing, and put in vetch for soil building, with rye as a nurse crop. In the spring, when the vetch was turned under, sudan was planted and grazed the first year. When fall came, the land was plowed again and planted to oats and Madrid sweetclover. After the oats were harvested, the Madrid came on and was cut for hay. There was no grazing that year.

By 1952, this thirteen acres could be irrigated from the water backed up by a small dam on the East Bosque. A sudan crop was harvested for hay, yielding about fifteen tons, worth $300. The Madrid had made 426 bales, worth $350, and the market value of the oats was $422.50. This made a total of $1072.50 from thirteen acres, or $82.50 per acre. The cost of irrigating this tract with sprinklers runs from $200 to $400, depending upon the amount and distribution of rainfall. In 1953, and again in 1954, alfalfa was grown on this field, increasing the fertility of the soil while producing big crops, yielding more than $1,000 per year. It was grazed lightly the first winter and heavily the second. Then the field was returned to its rotation of oats, Madrid sweetclover and sudan.

This program could have continued indefinitely, but in 1956, something new was tried. The area was planted to Caddo and Oklahoma switchgrass, cultivated in rows for seed production. Since there is water on two sides of the field, the roots will be down deeply enough for subirrigation by 1957, thus eliminating the expense of the sprinklers except on the high spots. By midsummer of 1956, there was a fine stand of grass, but it was too early to make any statements about yields. Switchgrass on irrigated land yields up to eleven tons of hay to the acre. Seed from these varities makes over two hundred pounds per acre and sells (1956) for $1.45 a pound. This little plot is now recognized as the best piece of land on the ranch, and if it is as successful as some of the others have been, it may turn out to be the biggest money-maker of all.

These are but a few of the many little corners along the creeks, from the quarter of an acre formerly in ragweed that is now producing $200 worth of Indiangrass seed, to the 68 acres of alfalfa on the Cureton place. But not one of these could begin to produce until cleared.

When a hay meadow is desired, it is wise to remove the trees and stumps, which interfere with the use of machinery. The added clearing cost is small when compared with the expense of operating the machinery. In the early days of the ranch, the wood was needed for so many purposes that it paid considerably more than half the cost of removing the trees.

To prepare the land for plowing is the most expensive operation, but it yields the greatest returns. Not only must the trees be removed, but the roots and stumps have to be

A fence of flat rock going into a pond is more durable than wire, and lessens the risk of drowning animals that may become entangled in wire fence.

An ideal fence with part of the wires on each side of the posts.

One of the Jackpot pastures.

ripped out to a depth of eighteen inches or two feet—and the ground is literally full of this stuff. Some old roots may be eight to ten inches in diameter. Everything is bulldozed that can be moved in that manner, and the trees and brush are pushed into the gullies. Usually, very good results may be obtained by seeding, following bulldozing, on heavy soil.

It takes time and effort, but "Hitting The Jackpot" pays!

Chapter 16

THE RANCH FAMILY
Martine Emert

EMPLOYEE WORKING conditions on Flat Top are among the best in the country. The owner shrewdly observed that hired men produce most efficiently where their working environment is favorable and where personal relations between employer and employee are congenial. He is instinctively kind and democratic, but he also knows that it is profitable to treat others as you want to be treated.

All of his life, he has been able to see beyond the troubles and problems of the immediate moment to the possibilities and promise of the future. He is dedicated to his objective, which is to produce the ideal pasture for the ideal cow—a permanent ranch dedicated to the improvement of Hereford cattle. His men have absorbed this same viewpoint.

The accomplishment of such an ideal can never be a one-man job; it requires complete teamwork. The men on Flat Top do not consider themselves employees working for a boss, but partners in an exciting and stimulating creative enterprise. Personality and a friendly attitude have had a great deal to do with establishing this relationship. Flat Top's owner has considered these men his personal friends, and their happiness has always been a matter of great concern to him. He goes over the ranch dressed for outdoor work, and discusses the ranch problems with them,

186

listening to their suggestions and encouraging them to use their own initiative. There is a lot of rugged hard work in ranching, and his sincere praise has helped many a man over a difficult job. Best of all, he has been able to transfer to them his enthusiasm and belief in the eventual eradication of the brush and weeds, the restoration of a complete cover of prairie grasses, and the establishment of a permanent ranch.

There is no labor trouble and almost no labor turnover at the Flat Top Ranch. There are good reasons for this situation.

In general, Flat Top salaries are higher than the customary wages for farm and ranch labor. In good years, a cash bonus is paid. One per cent of his yearly salary goes to the man with one year of service, 2 per cent for two years, and on up to 5 per cent for five years or over. Most men get 5 per cent.

Nearly everyone lives on the ranch property in houses for which they pay no rent. These homes are well located near the man's work and along the school bus route so the children can get to school easily. All bus stops have small shelters with low benches where the children can sit protected from the weather.

For most families, their ranch homes are the best they have ever known. Well built of frame or stone, these houses are modern, with baths, kitchen sinks, hot and cold running water, electricity, telephones, and butane gas. Few small farmers can afford these luxuries. Most of the utilities are free to families.

The families on the ranch obtain a considerable amount

187

of food free. A big garden, equipped for irrigation when necessary, is cultivated and the potatoes and beans and other vegetables are delivered to the employees' homes. Occasionally, a big beef is butchered, and the meat distributed to the ranch families.

The owner of Flat Top carries accident insurance on all of his men and pays half the cost of health insurance, besides arranging for low rates on health insurance for the families. Now when the wives or children are sick, they can go to the hospital, knowing that the cost is very little. The largest family on the ranch does not pay more than $7.04 a month of this insurance.

Since there are times on a ranch when the working hours must of necessity be long, liberal allowances are made for vacation, the only request being that time off should be taken when the work is slack.

The first employees hired on Flat Top were I. B. and Aline Roark. Jobs were scarce; they were broke, jobless, in debt, and besides, their seven-year-old son, Kenneth, needed his teeth straightened. Coming from a frugal background, they were awed at the apparent recklessness with which their new employer spent money tearing down old fences, wrecking ramshackle ranch buildings, rebuilding new fences, and constructing such durable and impressive rock barns and houses. They reasoned that their jobs would soon play out, and as a precaution against a day of need, they kept their milk cow and horse so they would have the foundation for a fresh start. The cow and horse died of old age, and I. B. and Aline are still at the ranch. For seventeen years, Aline has served as housekeeper and cook. Her skill

188

as a cook is vouched for by the many visitors who come from all parts of the world. She is hostess, in the absence of Mrs. Pettit, a responsibility she discharges with friendly efficiency. Aline is a vital part of everything about the ranch. She can do nearly all ranch jobs, including taking a hand at calving time, if necessary.

I. B. was first a cowhand, but later had the responsibility for the registered herd. Back about 1941, a little bull calf struck him as having something special. He groomed the little bull for the 1942 Fort Worth Livestock Show, and Flat Top had its first Grand Champion. This bull was the first great herd sire, *CP Tone,* whose descendants have been sold all over the world. After many years on the ranch, I. B. became Mr. Pettit's partner in a profitable feed mill in Walnut Springs, in 1954.

A few months after the Roarks arrived, Oland Hedrick was hired to build roads and dams, assist with the farming, plan the soil conservation work, and lay out terraces and contour farming operations on the cropland. Forty-three dams and 150 miles of road have been built. The largest dam of all is under construction.

Handling the heavy machinery is second nature to Oland, but his profound concern for the conservation of the soil and water has made him one of the most valued men on the ranch. As he became more keenly aware of the conservation problems of his neighbors and friends, as well as those of the ranch, he was elected supervisor of the Bosque Soil Conservation District, and encouraged farmers and ranchers in the county to adopt the conservation methods that were working so well on the ranch.

Oland has also made a very complete study of the grasses and other plants native to his area, not only for the purpose of identifying them, but to learn their growing habits and life histories, so that the valuable ones may be more easily and quickly re-established on the Flat Top pastures, and the poor ones eradicated. His concern for the grass is so great that (like Johnny Appleseed of old) he carries grass seed in his pocket to plant if he sees a little bare spot in his journeys over the ranch.

Bill Roberts, the manager, came to Flat Top in 1941. He is an expert cattleman and ranch manager. The men like him because he is a leader and not a boss. Bill works principally with the cattle, and few men are his equal in judging what a calf is going to turn into when it is a grown animal. He never misrepresents a sale. Flat Top policy is to give its buyers straight information about cattle, because it is satisfied customers that come back for more bulls. Bill's position as manager entails a great deal of planning, organization, and initiative. He figures very carefully how to make the cattle business pay even under the difficult circumstances of drought and low prices.

Three men now help Bill with the cattle: Clarence Stroud, Loyd Lundberg, and Hi Koonsman. Clarence and Leslie Stroud (brothers) came to work in 1942. Clarence came first to help with the grade cattle, but he particularly liked handling show animals.

When the ranch is not carrying on a show program, he tends the better animals, putting them into top condition. Flat Top Ranch owes many of its championship cups and ribbons to his careful work with the prize animals.

The Ranch Family

Loyd Lundberg came to the Flat Top Ranch in 1943, and Hi Koonsman a few years later. As pasture men, theirs is a very responsible task, for it is a real production job. A good pasture man has to know approximately when a calf may be expected, and on many cold nights, these men have to leave their warm beds to check the cows and assist at a birth.

Leslie Stroud has charge of the feed mill. He delivers the feed to the troughs, barns, and creep feeders. He checks the feeders at all times, keeps them clear of foreign material, and moves them when necessary. When the cattle were reduced because of the drought, Leslie took over the care of a small herd of white Yorkshire hogs, and they are flourishing under his care.

Ray Bennett cultivates the ranch garden, and as the vegetables, melons, and berries are ready for use, he gathers and distributes them to the families free of charge. Ray also looks after the cows that furnish milk to Mr. Pettit and his guests, to the Roarks, and to his own family. Mrs. Bennett makes the butter. Besides caring for the cows, the Bennetts raise chickens for their eggs, and keep a few guineas and peacocks.

Tillman Cain, who drives the big International truck and trailer, did a good deal of hauling for Flat Top for four years before he was employed full time on the ranch in 1947. The big truck has gone more than 125,000 miles, hauling cattle, feed, etc. all over the country, and is still in excellent condition. Also, he has good judgment in buying and selling. He frequently is sent to Illinois and other states to buy feed.

191

MARTINE EMERT

Two other men also have contributed much to Flat Top's development. These are W. M. (Pres) Preston, Mr. Pettit's secretary, and Floyd Rymer, who built most of the improvements on the ranch.

Mr. Preston started working for Mr. Pettit in August, 1931. Seven years later, Mr. Pettit made the first purchase of land in Bosque County and began the operation of the Flat Top Ranch. This became his principal interest, and he closed his Dallas office in 1952, consolidated all of his business activities in his office on the ranch, and Pres moved to Walnut Springs.

Pres is far more than an assistant or confidential secretary, for he and Mr. Pettit understand each other's points of view perfectly. He is the ranch accountant, and tax officials say his records are the most perfect they have ever seen.

Floyd Rymer built almost every structure of any consequence on the ranch, beginning at the time of the purchase of the first property in 1938. The house, the big barn, the sales barn, even the larger bridges and cattle guards are his work.

Floyd, in the opinion of other members of the ranch family, is a genius. He is carpenter, cabinet maker, plumber, electrician, mechanic, welder, machinist, and builder. Most of the improvements on Flat Top have been built without the guidance of an architect, Rock House being the exception. Mr. Pettit rather apologetically says, "I did use an architect on Rock House, but that was before I got well acquainted with Floyd." The more expensive Roberts' House was planned by Mrs. Roberts and built by Floyd without the help of an architect. Some of the members

192

of the ranch family say, "It is Mr. Pettit who has the ideas and Floyd who works out the mechanical end of the improvements." Floyd is a good shopper—a good buyer with judgment, who knows where to find the materials he needs at a bargain. Floyd now divides his time between the ranch and his business interests in Colorado.

These are the people who have been employees on the ranch for the greatest number of years. Others have worked on the ranch for shorter periods, and any who leave always want to come back. Each worker is responsible for planning and carrying out his work with a minimum of supervision, and takes pride in seeing that it is done efficiently and at the proper time. But more than that, each is proud to be a Flat Top hand. They are doing their part to build a stable, prosperous, and permanent agriculture.

Chapter 17

WATCHING FLAT TOP IMPROVE

FRANK REEVES

THE FIRST TIME I had an on-the-spot look at Flat Top Ranch was shortly after it was purchased by the present owner. My interest in the place had been whetted by a remark made by Bob Coody, an experienced West Texas rancher who had the place leased immediately prior to the time of its purchase.

Coody had asked if I knew the man who had purchased Flat Top Ranch. When I told him I did not, he said: "I am sorry for that man Pettit. He certainly has bought a lemon, and it will not take him long to find it out. I moved most of my cattle off the place before my lease was out to keep them from starving. If you had the feed, it would not be a good place to keep them."

Any direction you looked was most unimpressive from a ranch standpoint. The place looked shabby, worn, and depressing. You could not help but wonder what use could be made of the property. The open places were bare of grass, and the ugly signs of erosion caught and held the eye. There were some trees, but they appeared to be choked by a wide assortment of undergrowth. This brush was so thick in many places there was very little room for grass to grow. About the only class of livestock I could think of that might be adaptable to the place was Mexican goats.

194

When I left the ranch that afternoon, I was about convinced that Coody's off-hand description of the property was more accurate than exaggerated.

It has been my privilege and my pleasure to look over Flat Top Ranch many times each year since then. I have seen it in the summer, fall, winter, and spring. I have seen it during wet as well as during dry years. Regardless of the season or the occasion, I do not believe I ever visited the ranch that I did not recall Coody's description of the property. As the years went by, the changed conditions on the ranch fairly shouted at you that Coody had unwittingly misjudged the place.

Not too many years back, land was so plentiful and cheap in West Texas that it encouraged extravagant usage. Instead of making use of conservation practices for farm and ranch lands, the general practice was to get all you could out of the land and move to another location. Coody probably had more of this early-day attitude than he realized or others suspected. The same could be said about others who had occupied the place, because the physical scars were too deep and too numerous for one man to bring about in a short period of time.

The days of pioneering had long passed before Flat Top Ranch came under the ownership and direct supervision of its present owner, but since that time he has done a lot of pioneering—pioneering to rebuild fertility and productiveness of ranch land.

One of the first moves he made after buying the place was to surround himself with competent and dependable help. He was not one to delegate responsibilities to others

195

just to get them off his hands. He sought the advice of his men. His attitude made it easy for them to discuss the merit, or the lack of merit, of suggested projects.

His earnest desire to improve the property and make it a practical ranch was so obvious that it was infectious and inspirational to others. If a program worked out, he was quick to say, "We did it." If it failed, he was apt to say, "I made a bad guess."

It would be difficult to name an angle of farming, ranching, and cattle raising into which he did not venture, and more often than not, he did some pioneering, above and beyond the best of the time-proven practices, with the hope of making the best better.

He was ready to admit failure when an experiment did not turn out as he had hoped. Instead of being discouraged, he made these failures serve as guide posts for directing his efforts in other directions in his untiring efforts to map a program to make Flat Top Ranch a permanent ranch property.

His various ranch projects may have appeared somewhat revolutionary to some who did not have his inherent liking for the soil, but they were never visionary or started on the spur of the moment. He was more cautious than impulsive. His approach to his ranch problems utilized business practices he learned in other fields of endeavor. His experiments were on a comparatively small scale and were enlarged if they had merit and abandoned if they were impractical.

From the very first, he has endeavored to co-operate with nature to make Flat Top a better as well as a permanent ranch property. This has applied alike to water storage, water penetration, water utilization, soil conservation, soil productivity, and the growing of grasses.

Grasses are nature's contribution to man's welfare and existence. Some areas should never be used for the growing of farm crops, so our all-wise Creator covered them with grasses. Man does not eat grass directly, but he does eat a by-product from the grass—meat. No known plant or plants provide the delicious taste or the body building elements that come from meat.

Some densely populated areas where there is an ample supply of moisture depend upon farm crops for the human diet, but the living standards and life span of these people do not measure up to that of the people in the United States.

Grass-consuming animals provide the meat that is such a substantial part of the diet of the average American. If all grass were destroyed from the farms and ranches of the United States, famine would stalk like an ugly monster through the homes of ranchers, farmers, and city dwellers alike, who today are the envy of less fortunate people and nations. Posterity will gratefully remember our leaders who have worked to preserve and improve our natural resources and to make our farms and ranches produce more of the crops for the use and happiness of mankind that the Creator intended they grow.

The management at the ranch has made liberal use of recognized soil-building practices for the growing of grasses and farm crops. These grasses and farm crops were produced with the thought that they will be consumed by cattle for the production of super beef-producing animals.

These animals were produced, in the main, as seedstock for ranch use and distribution. Their production was predicated on their efficient beef-producing qualities in yielding a maximum amount of the more desirable cuts.

Since cattle can harvest range grasses in a very economical manner, considerable attention was given to the growing of range grasses. Overgrazing of the range was considered a cardinal sin at Flat Top Ranch. The growth of the more nutritious grasses was encouraged. The ranch has not been dilatory about trying new and improved grasses. Some of these produced worthwhile results. Others failed to come up to expectation due to moisture and soil conditions. To a certain extent, soil conditions can be modified and improved, and a lot of work has been done in that direction. Work has been done toward the storing and intelligent utilization of rainfall for the growing of more and better grasses.

Reseeding has been practiced extensively, and native grasses have played a worthwhile and major role in this work. Liberal use has been made of the best improved reseeding practices, along with some ranch-developed reseeding practices.

One such ranch-developed reseeding practice has been the cutting of pasture grass and scattering of the hay on areas that need reseeding. This hay makes an excellent mulch that holds the moisture; this encourages the seed germination, and then the hay serves as a nursemaid to the young grass plants until their root systems develop and take a firm hold in the soil.

Pettit has found this to be the quickest and easiest method

of providing a good stand of grass on areas where the soil bakes, cracks, and provides a difficult home for seedling grasses.

Almost every ranch and farm has some small plots of land that are not producing an average amount of grass. Often, such unproductive spots are on a hillside or the crown of a low hill or ridge. Once the turf has been damaged, these land sores have a tendency to enlarge and become cancerous, because erosion sets in with the lack of a grass covering to retard the runoff of rainwater.

Almost every ranch and farm has some areas that are brush-infested to the extent that a good crop of grass cannot be grown owing to the shade and the moisture-sapping tendencies of the brush and trees.

Flat Top had both of these kinds of unproductive land areas. I have watched, through the years, the disappearance of both the brush areas and the bare spots. The ranch has a simple and inexpensive method of eradicating these two uneconomical land areas. Anyone can apply this method any time there is a slack time in regular work. It can even be done piecemeal as a time saver.

The brush is cut, and as soon as this competition for plant food and moisture is eliminated, the native grasses come back. The brush is hauled to the bare area and scattered. It is not piled up thick. The brush will discourage livestock from walking over the bare spots. As the leaves and twigs from the brush begin to decay, they provide a much needed litter to the bare spots. The wind will bring in some grass seeds from the surrounding areas, but a few handfuls of grass seed scattered in the brush will speed the recovery

199

of the turf. The brush will also afford some protection to the young grass plants until the roots have time to penetrate into the soil. The brush mulch will also retard the water runoff and provide more water penetration. This is just one of the many little things being done to make Flat Top Ranch a permanent and profitable ranch property.

One of my most memorable visits to the ranch was made on October 30, 1950. The occasion was a field day program with about 375 representative ranchers participating. Charlie Pettit had then owned the ranch for a dozen years, and under his astute management, the progress made toward developing a permanent ranch was nothing less than amazing.

As the visitors drove through pasture after pasture, they saw hundreds of acres of pasture land covered with tall, dense-growing native pasture grasses with long, well-filled seed heads that nodded, billowed, and sparkled from the gentle breeze and the bright sunlight of a crystal clear October day. Without having it called to their attention, the trippers soon became conscious of the fact that they were seeing fewer trees and less brush but much more tall grass than on adjoining ranch lands.

This contrast was strikingly emphasized at a stop along a boundary fence between a Flat Top pasture and an adjoining ranch pasture. While the visitors ate a fresh warm sandwich and drank a cup of coffee from Jetton's unique barbecue truck, Pettit asked the visitors to note the difference in the grass growth in the adjoining pastures. He then explained that the Flat Top pasture had been sprayed with a weed killer early in the spring, and all cattle had been

200

Typical cottage home provided for Flat Top help.

The home of the ranch manager at Flat Top.

The main ranch house, showing four registered "lawn-mowers."

removed from the pasture in early June. The cattle had only been returned to the pasture a few days before the start of the tour.

The Flat Top pasture had a dense sod of big bluestem, Indiangrass, and little bluestem that stood from two to four feet in height, some of the Indiangrass even taller. There was an almost complete absence of weeds.

Just across the fence in the neighbor's pasture, there was a sparse growth of puny grass and a liberal infestation of unpalatable weeds. The presence of these weeds was convincing evidence that over-grazing is first evidenced by a curtailed supply of nourishing grasses and an increased supply of moisture-robbing weeds.

At another stop, Pettit pointed out an irrigated field of bottom land seeded to different grasses to provide protein-rich grazing during the winter months for his cattle. Water was being pumped from East Bosque Creek and distributed through light metal pipes.

From the very first, Pettit has focused his rebuilding program on the growing of more of the better grasses. He is firmly convinced that native grasses must play an important role in the economical production of beef. He has dedicated Flat Top Ranch to the improvement of Hereford cattle, and along with his pasture improvement work, he has combined a herd management program that is centered around environment, selection, and breeding, so that the two projects will support and complement each other to form a smooth-working economical whole.

He has developed some show herds of Herefords that have accomplished major winning at some of the better shows. This includes individuals in breeding-cattle classes, carloads of steers, and steers fed by club boys. Naturally, he is grateful that his cattle were able to win in strong competition. However, he is ever mindful of the fact that the eventual mission of Herefords is to produce beef in an economical manner. This, he insists, basically resolves itself into the utilization of pasture grasses, while retaining the qualifications for providing animals that will go into feed-lots and produce carcasses that will grade choice and prime. This means the carcasses must have conformation, color, covering, lining, and marbling—a proper blending of fat with lean meat to make it more tender.

To bring this about, he has been catering to ranchers who need several bulls in order to get uniformity, rather than fitting and showing his cattle and specializing in herd bull prospects.

The question asked most frequently during the field day program was not about the fine Herefords but, "How did you manage to grow so much grass?"

Flat Top Ranch never had much in the way of machinery until it was purchased by the present owner. Soon after he got possession, he started his development program, and this included an adequate supply of labor-saving equipment. He favored practical rather than elaborate machines.

Meager supplies of the "get-along" type of equipment were the general rule rather than the exception for a big majority of the neighboring ranchers and farmers. Some of the equipment put in by the ranch perhaps appeared to be too expensive for the use they visualized would be made of it. Some of the neighbors wondered out loud, "How can he afford it?" 202

They made the mistake of thinking only of the immediate future, whereas he was thinking of a long time, well-balanced development program that contemplated an efficiently operated permanent ranch property.

This long ahead look enabled him to visualize many uses for much of the equipment he was putting in, rather than just a seasonal use. He reasoned that by making the equipment serve more than one purpose, he would be able to distribute the original cost over a series of projects. Some of the development work he accomplished he could not have done profitably without an adequate supply of efficient labor-saving machinery. Many of the projects that were woven into the development of the ranch as a whole would have been too expensive had he relied on hand labor. The nationwide upturn in labor costs began soon after the ranch was purchased. There is nothing in the foreseeable future to indicate labor costs will ever return to the record low that many can recall. Such an economic cyclone would benefit no one, and it is not pleasant to contemplate such a possibility.

The ranch management, from the very first, adapted a policy of giving strict attention to its own individual problems. At the same time, it was fully conscious of the rights and needs of others, and a fixed policy, which was diligently adhered to, was adopted that tried to be a good neighbor by being co-operative. Pettit was ever mindful of local, regional, and state needs and programs. When extra labor was needed, an effort was made to find it near by.

On a visit to the ranch in the summer of 1955, I learned of a program that was started the previous winter and spring. It illustrates the dual use of equipment and the making use of local labor. Without either of these two ingredients, it would have been unsound economically.

During recent years there has been a growing tendency for putting out shade trees, in West Texas in particular. A great many of these trees have been native trees growing on uncultivated land. Nursery stocks did not have these trees to offer, so this work has involved a transplanting program of wild trees. The bigger and more reliable companies not only provided and replanted the trees, but they furnished a period of attention for the trees and guaranteed their growth.

Flat Top Ranch had some heavy equipment that was not very busy. There were some near-by neighbors, men known to be energetic, trustworthy, and reliable, who were anxious to get some extra work during the off season. The ranch had the trees, in fact there was an over-supply of trees in many places. These trees grew so close together that the ground was shaded too much for a good growth of grass.

The owner of Flat Top brought all of these segments together for one specific program. First, he made a deal with a reliable nursery to furnish it with trees. They gave specific instructions on just how the trees were to be uprooted, how much earth was to be taken out so as not to disturb the tree's root system, and how this earth was to be wrapped in burlap and made secure. The trees were paid for according to size. A crew of men was recruited among neighbors, and they went to work. These men used ranch equipment in the uprooting work and transportation of the trees. Some of the trees traveled about two hundred miles before they went back into the ground.

Where did Flat Top Ranch profit from such a deal? A reasonable charge was figured for the use of the ranch equipment. In addition to the trees that were uprooted and moved away, there was an understanding about a certain amount of brush removal work to be done at the same time. Shapely young trees were left standing, and in years to come, they will be available and accessible if they are ever needed. The ranch will have a much better growth of grass where the trees and brush were growing. A little here and a little there made a satisfactory whole in the ranch development work.

Pettit worked in another practice that has demonstrated its value in different ways. Instead of completely filling the holes where the trees were removed, he left a shallow hole. These holes will not be a menace to the ranch livestock, but they will catch runoff water and encourage its penetration into the soil instead of running into branches and creeks and eventually ending up in the Gulf of Mexico.

This underground storage of water in the soil means extra grass, and extra grass means better grazing for cattle and more pounds of beef produced in an economical manner.

I probably have seen as many ranches and as many beef animals in the past quarter century as any man in America. My job has made this not only possible but necessary. One of the great rewards of my job as a range reporter and livestock editor is the regular opportunity to observe the continuing improvement of certain ranches. In no case that I can recall has the improvement of the range, the hay meadows, the water system, the houses, barns, fences, and the cattle been so constant as at Flat Top.

However, it is no different from other ranch lands in that area of the Lampasas Cut Plain so far as natural physical conditions are concerned. The ranch has its quota of rough low hills, narrow valleys, and rolling areas. The soil varies from a few inches to several feet in depth, depending on the whims of Mother Nature and the ranching practices of current and past owners since the county was settled about one hundred years ago. The soils are no more and no less fertile than neighboring ranch lands. Climatic conditions are identical with the usual seasonal variables, plus vagaries of weather conditions common to this part of Central Texas from year to year.

The primary difference between Flat Top and the nearby ranches is in the foresight and the managerial ability of my friend, Charlie Pettit. He has never lost sight of the importance of grass in developing his livestock enterprise. As I drive through the rank and dense growth of grass at Flat Top, it is easy to think of Ingall's ode to grass that begins: "Grass is the forgiveness of nature, her constant benediction." And ends: "It yields no fruit in earth or air, and yet should harvest fail for a single year famine would depopulate the world."

The harvest has not failed a single year at Flat Top, despite more than five and a half years of short to very short rainfall. Flat Top has met the tests of time and drought and has clearly earned the right to be known as A Permanent Ranch.

Appendix A

FLAT TOP VEGETATION

B. W. ALLRED

Native Grasses

Tall wheatgrass
Western wheatgrass
Big bluestem *
Bushy bluestem
Little bluestem *
Silver bluestem
Oldfield threeawn A
Purple threeawn
Red threeawn
Eastern gama
Hairy grama
Sideoats grama *
Tall grama *
Texas grama
Buffalograss
Mat sandbur A
Hooded windmillgrass
Tumble windmillgrass
Showy Chloris A
Hairy crabgrass A
Texas crabgrass A
Barnyardgrass A
Goosegrass
Canada wildrye *
Virginia wildrye *

Fall witchgrass
Ozarkgrass A
Carolina jointtail
Green muhly
Seep muhly
Blue panicum
Filly panicum
Gaping panicum
Halls panicum
Hellers panicum
Scribners panicum
Switchgrass *
Vine-mesquite
Florida paspalum
Fringeleaf paspalum
Sand paspalum
Carolina canarygrass A
Annual bluegrass A
Texas bluegrass
Tumblegrass
Indiangrass *
Hairy dropseed
Hidden dropseed
Meadow dropseed
Poverty dropseed A

207

Gummy lovegrass
Mourning lovegrass
Purple lovegrass
Red lovegrass
Sand lovegrass
Stinkgrass A
Tumble lovegrass
Texas cupgrass
Sixweeks fescue A
Curlymesquite
Little barley A
Foxtail barley
Prairie Junegrass
Red sprangletop A

Puffsheath dropseed A
Sand dropseed
Tall dropseed
Whorled dropseed
Texas wintergrass *
Hairy tridens
Purpletop
Rough tridens
White tridens
Prairie trisetum
Broadleaf uniola
Also there are several sedges, rushes, and cattail.

* The most important forage-producing grasses.
A—Annual grasses.

Grasses Introduced from Foreign Countries

King Ranch bluestem
Japanese brome A
Rescuegrass A
Smooth brome
Bermudagrass
Sorghum A
Rye A
A—Annuals.

Orchardgrass
Suiter fescue
Kentucky fescue
Dallisgrass
Johnsongrass
Barley A
Oats A

Native and Introduced Legumes

Groundplum milkvetch
Nuttall milkvetch A
Texas senna
Eastern redbud
Showy partridgepea A
Atlantic pidgeonwings

Texas bluebonnet A
Button clover I A
Alfalfa I
Madrid sweetclover (biennial)
Yellow neptunia
Lambert crazyweed

208

Appendix

Bigtop dalea
Black dalea
Purple dalea
Silktop dalea
Illinois bundleflower
Prairie bundleflower
American licorice
Western indigo
Trailing ratany
Deervetch A

Commanche Peak prairieclove
Purple prairieclover
White prairieclover
Mesquite
Edible scurfpea
Slimleaf scurfpea
Wild-alfalfa
Catclaw sensitivebriar
Hairy vetch I A
Leavenworth vetch

A—Annuals.   I—Introduced.

Common Forbs

Wild onion
Anemone
Pussytoes
Goldenweed
Dogbane
Pricklepoppy P
Sagewort
Milkweed
Blue aster
Heath aster
Prairie-bishop
Poppymallow
Bellflower
Shepherdspurse
Centaurea
American basketflower
Chervil
Lambsquarters
Goldaster
Snow-on-the-mountain P
Evax P

Thistle
False garlic
Bullnettle P
Dayflower
Rainlily
Coreopsis
Croton P
Carrot
Larkspur
Buttonweed
Dychoriste
Dogweed
Blacksamson
Engelmanndaisy
Horseweed fleabane P
Philadelphia fleabane
Wild-buckwheat
Eryngo
Snow-on-the-prairie P
Phlox
Plantain

209

Evolvulus
Gaillardia
Gaura
Geranium
Gilia
Gumweed P
Common broomweed P
Sunflower
Bluets
Morninglory
Rockdaisy
Pinweed
Gayfeather
Flax
Mallow
Falsemallow
Hoarhound P
Evening primrose
Sundrops
Cactus P
Oxalis
Nailwort
Penstemon

Milkwort
Knotweed and smartweed
Buttercup
Prairiegentian
Coneflower
Dock
Sage
Skullcap
Groundsel
Rosinweed
Bushsunflower
Blue-eyed grass
Nightshade
Goldenrod
Globemallow
Queensdelight
Greenthread
Spiderwort
Nettle
Verbena
Ironweed P
Western ragweed P
There are several hundred more forbs on the ranch.

P—forbs that are the most bothersome pests.

Some of the Most Common Trees, Shrubs, and Vines

Pecan
Jerseytea
Hackberry
Redbud
Clematis
Walnut
Juniper (Ashe and redberry)

Sumac
Rose
Willow
Greenbriar
Trumpetflower
Poisonivy
Cedar elm

Appendix

Cottonwood

Bur oak

Blackjack oak

Live oak

Spanish oak

Shinnery oak

Post oak

Mustang grape

Yucca

Pricklyash

Zexmenia

Skunkbush

Appendix B

THE CONTRIBUTORS

Louis Bromfield was a distinguished novelist, farmer, and conservationist. He was a native of Ohio and was educated at Cornell, Ohio Northern University, and Columbia. His college work was interrupted by World War I, and he was overseas 1917–19, with the American Ambulance Corps, attached to the French Army.

During his earlier writing years, he lived abroad much of the time. His novel, *Early Autumn,* won the Pulitzer prize in 1926, but *The Rains Came* is considered by many to be his best novel. His own favorite of all his fiction was *The Strange Case of Miss Annie Spragg.* He was a prolific writer, and in addition to his novels, wrote several plays and many articles on music, economics, and international politics.

About twenty years ago, Louis came to his beloved Ohio hills and valleys. He became an ardent soil conservationist, and his home place, Malabar Farm, became one of the truly great demonstrations of the value of soil and water conservation in America. His two most popular books of recent years, *Pleasant Valley* (1945) and *Malabar Farm* (1948), are partially autobiographical and set forth many of his experiences on the farm. He was vice president of the Friends of the Land and a willing lecturer and writer on conservation. His enthusiasm influenced many other farmers, ranchers, and businessmen to lend their active support to the conservation movement.

His untimely death on March 18, 1956, interrupted his last joint literary-conservation project—the editing of this book about his friend Charlie Pettit's ranch. Fortunately, the two chapters which he had agreed to contribute were finished. They were among the last, if not the last, pieces of writing he did. Louis Bromfield was a congenial companion, a talented writer, an entertaining speaker, a crusader for a permanent agriculture in America, and a conservation farmer. His contributions to literature and agriculture will live. (J.C.D.)

CHARLES CLINTON BOOTH, grandson of Charles Pettit, was born in 1931 in Dallas, Texas. He attended Washington and Lee University in Lexington, Virginia, where he received a B.A. in economics in June, 1953. Clint majored in geology at the University of Texas where he received an M.A. degree in June, 1956. He was a member of Sigma Gamma Epsilon, national earth sciences fraternity. His thesis was "Geology of Chalk Mountain Quadrangle, Bosque, Erath, Hamilton, and Somervell Counties, Texas." He spent the summers of 1954 and 1955 doing the field work on this area adjacent to Flat Top Ranch. Clint is now (1956) employed in Corpus Christi, Texas, as a geologist with the Atlantic Refining Company. (B.W.A.)

B. W. (BILL) ALLRED was born in Moab, Utah and reared on a Utah ranch. He has B.S. and M.S. degrees from Utah

213

Agricultural College, and later took additional graduate work at the University of Nebraska. He ran sheep on the Red Desert in Wyoming and has worked with other farms and ranches in which he was personally interested. At the present time he owns a livestock or, as he prefers to call it, "a grass farm" in western Maryland. After serving as a county agent in Colorado, he joined the Soil Conservation Service staff in 1935 as a range conservationist. He worked with the ranchers in both the Northern Great Plains region (1935–1945) and the Southern Great Plains region (1945–1953) before being promoted to ranch planning specialist in the Washington office of the Soil Conservation Service in 1953. He is a past president of the American Society of Range Management and a charter member of the Washington (D. C.) Westerners. He collects Western Americana, specializing in the books on range life.

He is the author of *Range Conservation Practices for the Great Plains* (USDA Miscellaneous Publication No. 410, 1940); *Practical Grassland Management* (San Angelo, Texas, and Danville, Ohio, 1950); joint editor of *Dynamics of Vegetation,* (New York, Wilson and Co., 1949); "The Management of the Range Land of the West" in *Water and Man* by Forman and Fink (Columbus, Ohio, Friends of the Land, 1950); "Influence of Shrub Invasion of United States Range Lands" in *Proceedings* of the Sixth International Grassland Congress, Vol. 1 (Pennsylvania State College, Pa., 1952); joint author of *Grass for Conservation in the Southern Great Plains* (Farmers Bulletin 2093, 1955); and over 400 articles and book reviews in newspapers, trade journals, and professional magazines. (J.C.D.)

Appendix

MARTINE EMERT is associate professor of history and geography at Texas Christian University at Fort Worth, Texas. She was born in Kansas and earned the A.B., M.A., and Ph.D. degrees at the University of California at Berkeley. She taught at her Alma Mater, at the University of New Mexico, and at Adams State College, Alamosa, Colorado, before joining the faculty at TCU. Dr. Emert is an enthusiastic conservationist and she has followed with much interest the step-by-step development of the grassland venture at Flat Top. She is a Phi Beta Kappa and has won many scholastic honors and awards but she is proudest of the State of Texas, 1953 Conservation Award for Unselfish Service. She has traveled much in Latin America and is a member of the Southwest Social Science Association, the Texas Geographical Society and the Soil Conservation Society of America. (B.W.A.)

J. C. (JEFF) DYKES is a native Texan and was reared in the bluestem belt in Dallas County. His father, George, was a neighbor of William Cureton on the East Fork of the Bosque in the eighties and it is quite likely his brand once grazed what is now Flat Top range. According to the late Hugh Cureton, George Dykes brought the first improved hogs, Duroc Jerseys, to Bosque County and the Curetons bought their breeding stock from him. They raised the "red Dykes hogs" as long as they lived on the East Bosque. Jeff was graduated from Texas A. & M. in 1921 in agricultural engineering. He did graduate work at Colorado Agricultural College and at Texas A. & M. After eight years of teaching vocational agriculture in Texas high schools, he became pro-

215

fessor of agricultural education at Texas A. & M., a position
he held until he joined the staff of the Soil Conservation
Service in 1935. For the past fourteen years, he has been
in the SCS Washington office as deputy chief and assistant
administrator. He is a fellow of the Soil Conservation Society of America. He is a member of the Texas, Kansas
(life), Montana, and Wyoming Historical Societies and is a
charter member and chairman of the Publications Committee of the Washington Westerners. He has been an associate editor of *The Brand Book,* the official monthly publication of the Chicago Westerners, since 1950. Jeff is an
ardent collector of Western Americana, and his library now
exceeds 6,000 volumes. He is one of the nation's outstanding
authorities on Western books. He is the author of *Billy the
Kid: The Bibliography of a Legend* (University of New
Mexico Press, 1952); and introduction to Pat Garrett's *The
Authentic Life of Billy the Kid* (University of Oklahoma
Press, 1954) and numerous articles and papers on Western
books and conservation plus many book reviews for newspapers, magazines, and society quarterlies. (B.W.A.)

G. OLAND HEDRICK was born on a farm twelve miles southwest of Cleburne, Texas, April 25, 1901. He attended a
one-room, one-teacher school four years and then finished
grade and high school at Walnut Springs, Texas.

Oland worked four years for the Ford agency at Walnut
Springs, Texas, including the operation of its demonstration farm for two years.

Perhaps his most important experience prior to coming

to Flat Top came during the twelve years he worked for the Bosque County Commissioner, Precinct No. 2, building and maintaining roads.

Oland has been on his present job with Mr. Pettit since January 1, 1939. (B.W.A.)

W. B. (BILL) ROBERTS was born at Eden Mills, Ontario, Canada, in 1909, and is of Scotch-English descent. He received his primary education in a one-room, one-teacher school, and then attended Milton High School two years and Guelph High School two years.

Bill worked two years at Sni-A-Bar Shorthorn Cattle Farms, Grain Valley, Missouri, where he had the privilege of observing livestock experimental work carried on by the farm in co-operation with the U.S.D.A. and the University of Missouri.

One year on the 17,000-acre Heart's Delight Farm, Chazy, New York, provided an opportunity to work with and observe the management of beef cattle, dairy cattle, sheep, hogs, chickens, turkeys, and draft and light horses. There was also a fish hatchery and a game department at Heart's Delight.

During the ten years he worked for Mathers Brothers, Mason City, Illinois, Bill received valuable training in farming and livestock from these University of Illinois graduates. One had majored in animal husbandry and was a graduate of Chicago Veterinary College, while the other had majored in fields and crops.

He had his first experience with irrigation farming while

217

managing the Dunridge Ranch, San Antonio, Texas, for two years. Both Shorthorn and Hereford cattle were raised at Dunridge.

He spent one year at Essar Ranch, San Antonio, Texas, where he got limited experience with Angus and Brahman cattle and additional experience in handling Herefords.

Bill has been a resident manager at Flat Top since 1941. He is an excellent Hereford judge and a cattle breeding expert. He has the confidence of many ranchers throughout the country and so great is it on the part of some that they no longer go to the expense of visiting Flat Top to buy bulls. It is not uncommon for a Hereford breeder to telephone the ranch and ask Bill Roberts to select a number of bulls to be shipped to him unseen. The repeat orders after such selections are further evidence of the esteem in which Bill and his employer, Charlie Pettit, are held in Hereford circles. (L.B.)

WILLIAM R. VAN DERSAL was born in Portland, Oregon and received his early education in the Portland schools. He was graduated from Reed College there in 1929. From 1929 to 1935 Van studied and taught at the University of Pittsburgh. He received his master's degree in botany in 1931 and his doctor's degree in 1933. He became a forester for the Soil Conservation Service in 1935 but transferred to the Washington office in 1936 as assistant chief of the Biology Division. In 1942 he was made chief of the Personnel Management Division. In 1946 he was made chief of operations for the Pacific region with headquarters at Portland, Oregon. He came back to the SCS Washington office as assistant administrator for management in 1954. He received the Rockefeller Public Service Award for 1956–57, and is currently engaged in a study of the administration of conservation activities in Canada, Australia, New Zealand, and the United States. Van plans to return to his SCS job in October, 1957. He collects books on plants and wildlife. He is the author of: *Native Woody Plants of the U. S., Their Erosion Control and Wildlife Values* (USDA Misc. Publication 303, 1939); *Ornamental American Shrubs* (Oxford University Press, 1942); *The American Land* (Oxford University Press, 1943); with Edward H. Graham, *The Land Renewed* (Oxford University Press, 1946); *Wildlife for America* (Oxford University Press, 1949); and *Water for America* (Oxford University Press, 1956); and numerous articles and papers on wildlife, ecology, conservation, and management in newspapers, magazines, and scientific journals. (J.C.D.)

FRANK REEVES grew up on a small stock farm near Graham, in Young County, Texas. In one way or another he has been interested in and associated with ranching practices, the breeding and feeding of beef cattle, and their marketing all his life.

He was with the SMS Ranch with headquarters at Stamford, Texas, for twelve years. He was assistant manager to the late Frank S. Hasting, who established the practice of selling feeder cattle in carload lots by correspondence to corn belt feeders. He became acquainted with many of the ranch's customers and made numerous trips to the corn belt to check on conditions among the feeders. He regularly attended the Chicago International Fat Stock Show.

For the past 28 years Frank has been with the Fort Worth *Star Telegram* as a reporter of livestock news, as market reporter on the Fort Worth Stockyards, and as livestock editor. His paper believes in and features the livestock industry, and as a result it is widely read in the ranch country throughout the Southwest. In no small measure Frank is responsible for the popularity and the big circulation of the *Star Telegram* among ranch folks.

For a number of years he has devoted his entire time to ranch field days and tours, livestock shows, sales, and conventions, which he has reported for the *Star Telegram*. He writes a daily column, "Chuck-Wagon," devoted to happenings in livestock circles.

Each fall he makes a trip through the corn belt states to talk with feeders, farmers, bankers, and livestock commission firms to get and report their views about crop conditions, prices for feeders, cattle supplies, and fat cattle prices which he passes on to the readers of the *Star Telegram* in the range country.

Frank is an ardent photographer and has been able to combine his hobby for pictures with his writing about people and the livestock industry.

He is the author of a Highland Hereford Association illustrated booklet, *The Story of the Highlands* (Marfa, Texas, 1936), and of the *Hacienda de Atotonilco* (Yerbanis, Durango, Mexico, 1936), the illustrated account of the famed Raymond Bell Ranch. The Bell Ranch booklet was printed in both English and Spanish.

A few years ago, during the Southwestern Exposition and Fat Stock Show at Fort Worth, Texas, Reeves was given a surprise recognition dinner and presented with an automobile purchased by friends and livestock breed associations from many states.   (J.C.D.)

INDEX

Agricultural Stabilization and Conservation Committee: 56
Albany, Texas: 115f.
Alberta, Canada: 117, 119
Alexander, F. W.: 116f.
Alfalfa: 22, 34, 38, 68, 77, 83, 87f., 90, 104ff., 136f., 146f., 160, 184
Allred, B. W.: 128
American Agriculture: 15
American bison: 158
American continent: 29
American farmer: 9
American grassland: 29
American heartland: 29
American Hereford Association: 74, 112, 117
Ammonites: 25
Annual broomweed: 52
Antelope: 21f., 66, 95, 105, 141f., 147f., 158, 160
Archer County, Texas: 14, 108, 110, 134
Argentine: 122

Armadillos: 155, 157
Aspens: 154
Austin, Texas: 97
Austrian winter peas: 40, 86

Balance of Nature: 159ff.
Barbed wire: 97
Barley: 34, 86, 105
Barn: 162; breeding 70; bull, 40; calving, 70, 163; corrugated iron, 164, 167; feed, 163f., 167f.; rock, 165, 168f.; sale, 168; utility, 168; weaning, 168
Barry, Colonel Buck: 95, 140, 144, 156
Bass: 21; large mouth, 153
Beans: 155, 160, 188
Bear: 141
Beaver: 154, 158f.
Beeville, Texas: 123
Bell, Arthur: 33
Belt, Montana: 117
Bennett, Mrs.: 191
Bennett, Ray: 191

www.ingramcontent.com/pod-product-compliance
Lightning Source LLC
Chambersburg PA
CBHW030915090426
42737CB00007B/205